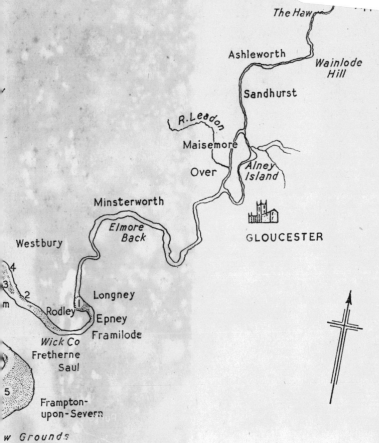

The Mythe

The Haw

Ashleworth

Wainlode
Hill

Sandhurst

R. Leadon

Maisemore

Over

Alney
Island

Minsterworth

Elmore
Back

GLOUCESTER

Westbury

4
3
2
m

Rodley

Longney

Epney

Framilode

Wick Co

Fretherne

Saul

5

Frampton-
upon-Severn

w Grounds

idge

nchcombe
Hill

SEVERN TIDE

THE BORE APPROACHING GLOUCESTER, OCTOBER 1945

SEVERN TIDE

by

BRIAN WATERS

*Illustrated with
16 pages of photographs*

LONDON

J. M. DENT & SONS LTD

C 130/2 m

CONTENTS

ILLUSTRATIONS

THE WILD DUCK

Sickled in the evening sky
A flight of wild duck on the wing;
I have heard a wild duck cry
As though they all would sing,
For at his cry they whirred and flew
Into one mighty string.
Then at the harsh note
Of one commanding throat,
Each from his flank
Divided rank to rank.
For now on Severn's bank they each did deem
Some honour due unto the ancient stream;
As into two bright flanks of bold divide,
Rank behind rank they flew across the tide.
The Severn saw, and in her mirror bright
Signalled her calm delight,
For twice a thousand bodies strong
On outstretched wing did sing this song—
'Severn, Severn, thou dost flow
Into the West whither we go
To seek our bed in the fiery red
Of this evening's golden glow.'

I. THE BORE

Between March and April the Severn Bore is at its biggest, elvers at their thickest, and spring at its earliest. Below Gloucester the river flows between steep banks ten feet high until it is overwhelmed by all the strength and fury of the sea.

You stand and hold your breath, for in this land which holds neither mirages nor volcanoes the river is flowing backwards, as a great wave a hundred yards broad and nine feet high comes rolling up the river. It is like a weir frozen to the smoothness of ice, for the water instead of falling advances, and might for a split second appear to be still, except that the angry ostrich plumes of white spray, as they lash themselves against the top of the river bank, show with what speed the Bore advances. This apparent lack of motion in the wave fascinates the eye with the desire to arrest its motion, if only for an instant, to comprehend this magic of nature's sleight of hand.

It is a great moment when you watch the Bore turn a bend of the river for the first time, yet before you have fully comprehended its wonder, the great wave is casting its plumes at your feet. These feathers are white as they leave the wave and shade to muddy sepia as they scour the grasses of the bank, filling your nostrils with the faint but certain smell of the sea, which a moment earlier scented the fragrance of a spring shower. The Bore rolls on with the speed of a horse at a canter, and behind it rolls the turbulence of a tide in flood running at sixteen miles an hour, carrying with it logs of timber, the carcasses of animals, and any other trifles that have lain in the broad path of the tideway.

The Bore received its baptismal name from the Saxons, who named it *bara*, the wave, the Severn tide in its turn gave to the Saxon settlers of this region the tribal name of Hwicci, the men of the tidal creek. In the sixteenth century the Bore was known as the Hygre, and the prose of William Camden

*

touches the fervour of poetry when in his *Britannia* he writes in praise of the river: 'To all of which may be added, in honour of this county [Gloucestershire], the river Severn; than which there is not any in the land that hath a broader channel, swifter stream or more plenty of fish. There is in it a daily rage and boisterousness of waters, which I know not whether I may call a gulph or whirlpool, casting up the sands from the bottom, and rowling them into heaps, it floweth with a great torrent, but loses its force at the first bridge. Sometimes it overfloweth its banks and wanders a great way into the neighbouring plaines, and then returneth back as conqueror of the land. That vessel is in great danger that is stricken on the side. The watermen us'd to it, when they see this Hygre coming do turn the vessel, and cutting through the midst of it avoid its violence.'

The bold imagery of Michael Drayton gives a more intimate, if cruder, picture of the Bore:

With whose tumultuous waves,

Shut up in narrower bounds, the Hygre wildly raves ;
And frights the straggling flocks, the neighbouring shores to fly
Afar as from the main it comes with hideous cry.
And on the angry front the curling foam doth bring,
The billows 'gainst the banks when fiercely it doth fling;
Hurls up the slimy ooze, and makes the scaly brood
Leap madding to the land affrighted from the flood;
O'erturns the toiling barge, whose steersman doth not launch,
And thrusts the furrowing beak into her ireful paunch:
As when we haply see a sickly woman fall
Into a fit of that which we the mother call,
When from the grieved womb she feels the pain arise,
Breaks into grievous sighs, with intermixed cries
Bereaved of her sense ; and struggling still with those
That 'gainst her rising pain their utmost strength oppose,
Starts, tosses, tumbles, strikes, turns, touses, spurns, and sprawls,
Casting with furious limbs her holders to the walls ;
But that the horrid pangs torment the grieved so,
One might well muse from whence this sudden strength should grow.

The Bore comes with the spring tides, and for this reason many landsmen and people unacquainted with the river imagine that the Bore is to be seen once a year only in the spring. A spring tide, however, is the highest tide in any lunar month, and the top of the spring occurs three tides after the full or new moon, when both sun and moon act in the same direction. Bores come every month for several days and nights either side of the top of the spring, and the finest bores are to be seen on the top of the spring nearest to the spring and autumn equinoxes. Then the tide may be over thirty-one feet, or even in exceptional years as high as thirty-two feet four inches, but any tide over thirty feet makes a very fine showing on the river reaches below Gloucester. Severn tide is measured by high water at the river port of Sharpness. Below Sharpness the Severn broadens to an average width of two miles for ten miles, until the Beachley peninsula curves towards Aust Cliff, where the bed of the river narrows to less than a mile. This area land-locks the highest tide in Europe and one of the highest in the world.

The spring tides surge past Sharpness up the winding, gently shelving bed of the river, and the wave which was three feet as it passed Sharpness, instead of diminishing, gains height as it pushes its way up the narrowing bed of the river, until it reaches a height of nine feet at Stonebench. A few minor rapids are taken in its stride, but some idea of the gradualness of the ascent may be seen in the Gloucester–Sharpness canal, which links these two places, uninterrupted by any lock, as it halves the mileage of dangerous river passage.

The Bore is a great traveller and will cover forty miles of river on a great tide in two and a half hours, the distance from Sharpness to Tewkesbury Lock. Under the most favourable conditions of wind, tide, and water, tides have been recorded as far inland as Worcester, some sixty-six miles by river from the open sea, only a little less than a third of the total length of the Severn. Daniel in his *Rural Sports* records the extraordinary incident how, 'in the Severn, near Worcester, a man bathing, was struck, and actually received his death wound, from a sword fish, *Xiphias gladius*. The fish was caught immediately afterwards, so that the fact was ascertained beyond a doubt.'

As might be imagined, the tide has begun to ebb from the mouth of the river long before it can make its presence felt so far inland. The Bore, indeed, does not reach Gloucester until as hour after high water at Sharpness and by this means Gloucester folk reckon on the arrival of their tide, for it takes the wave nearly two hours to cover this portion of its journey. Thus when the Bore reaches Framilode it is high water at Sharpness and Framilode's high water coincides with the arrival of the wave below Gloucester. Some allowance has to be made in these calculations, for a strong north-easterly wind may delay the Bore's arrival by ten minutes, and many a punctual spectator has missed seeing the Bore through the wind being in the opposite direction. The Bore is at its finest on such occasions with the wind behind it as it rolls up the river after a rainless spell, for with the water at its lowest the wave makes a great showing as it rolls over the shallows.

The wave is followed by such a volume of water that high water on Gloucester's reach of river seems to be attained with the impact of the Bore's arrival, but the tide flows on, adding inch by inch another foot or so after the wave has passed. The paradox of the tide ebbing out of the mouth of the river, while the Bore surges upstream in apparent contradiction of the laws of nature, may be explained by the analogy of a ball rolling up the incline of a skittle alley while the hand of the bowler rests idly at his side. Nevertheless, the tide in passing almost imperceptibly loses pace, until after fifty minutes it comes to a standstill, and for five minutes the river is motionless as a pond.

The Bore, as it approaches Gloucester, divides on striking the Lower Parting at Alney Island. Half the wave turns eastwards, towards the city, while the other half runs north-wards to Maisemore. The Gloucester wave is soon confronted by Llanthony Weir, which it overwhelms at the cost of its pride, but not of its fury, and those who stand on Westgate Bridge see a sadly diminished wave sweep beneath them. From Westgate Bridge the road crosses the island to where Thomas Telford, in deference to the tide, replaced the old bridge of Over by crossing Maisemore River in a single span. Although the railway bridge stands immediately in front of it this elevation is a fine place from which to observe the Bore, though nothing is lost by going a mile up river and standing on the bridge of Maisemore.

Alney is a flat, fertile pasture, almost uninhabited except for the cluster of houses by Westgate Bridge, for at times of freshwater flood the island is almost entirely under water. The railway and road embankments, crossing the island, act as dams, which greatly hinder the floods from the upper valley from escaping to the sea. If Alney had stood on higher ground it might have been the site of the greatest city in England, for it is surrounded by seven and a half miles of river. As it is, Alney is responsible for Gloucester standing where it does, for in dividing the strength of the greatest natural obstacle in Britain it provided an easy and safe crossing of the two streams.

The Maisemore River is only half as long as the Gloucester stream, and, with its water unpolluted by the city, is preferred by the salmon and the elver. The elver travels on the tide in the early days of spring. Years ago the parents who spawned him left this, or some other river of western Europe, never to return. These eels crossed the Atlantic, descending to a depth of five hundred fathoms off the continental shelf of Central America, to lay and fertilize their progeny, after which they sank into oblivion, for no adult eel has ever been caught returning to the river from the sea and an absolutely mature female eel has yet to be seen. The larva of the eel moves gradually upwards and eastwards; for three years the ocean is his cradle, during which time he remains a larva. In this state he grows and he travels; after two years he is in the middle of the Atlantic and is about two inches long. By his third summer he has grown another inch and as winter comes on he turns into an elver. He is now nearing our coasts and is thirsty for fresh water. The ocean which has carried him so far sweeps him and his kind into the mouth of the Severn in the early days of spring. They enter the river in great droves, which become thicker as the river narrows. Elvers are fished for the length of Severn tide, from Lydney to

Tewkesbury, by enthusiastic amateurs, and many tons of them are caught by riverside men in the months of March and April. Maisemore, being near to Gloucester, is a great place for the elverer, for he is a wise fisherman who catches his elvers near home.

Of all fishing tackle the elver-net is the most pleasing to the eye, for it has an almost Chinese line of graceful, box-like angularity. About three feet long, two feet wide, and twenty inches deep, the net is built on a cradle of willow at the end of a five-foot pole. This framework is covered in cheesecloth and, unlike other nets, the elver-net is stiff and rigid. These nets are home-made, yet all conform to a uniform pattern. Nets are fastened mouth downwards over the backs of cycles as fishermen go forth to meet the ebb of the tide, for unless he is punctual the fisherman might as well stay at home. A night tide is often the more favoured as the light of a lantern will lure the elvers to the net. As the tide dwindles towards its ebb, a few elverers dip their nets in the river, and half of them know that they are wasting their time. The more experienced set about making themselves comfortable, and the oldest hands even take a spade with them to cut seats for themselves in the river bank.

The turn of the tide is almost imperceptible, but it is abrupt. Elver-nets are dipped in the water with their backs to the current. The elver-net is submerged for half a minute, and when raised a score of elvers are seen squirming in the bottom. They are exactly the colour of the dun cheesecloth and, but for their squirming in spirals, they would pass unnoticed. This first dip the experienced elverer will hardly trouble to land. The second draught will yield perhaps a pint and will be decanted into the waiting pail; from now the hauls will rise to quarts or even gallons, or they may remain at modest pints, according to the quality of the tide.

Occasionally two pailfuls may be hauled in on one net, and under such conditions it will only be a matter of minutes before the fisherman has landed as much as he can carry home. The elverer is not greedy but he likes a lot, and many are not satisfied until they have caught a hundredweight. There is a ready sale for the fish, and the astute amateur may make on a single tide as much money as he will earn in a week at his regular occupation. Once in the pail the elvers froth like newly drawn beer, and a few inches of elvers will quickly form an inch of foam. The elvers squirm up the sides of the pail in their ineffectual attempts to escape. In their writhings the fish display their herd instinct to a remarkable degree, for half a dozen or more will weave themselves into a pattern like a leaping tongue of flame that tapers to a point and then subsides. This curious effect is enhanced by the translucent quality of the elver, tinged as he is in the sunlight with a dim sea-green sheen. Elvers come to the net quickly, and within an hour of the turn of the tide the hauls fall off from quarts to pints and from pints to teacupfuls, down to a shingling of half a dozen or more elvers, which are thrown out on to the bank from where they wriggle back to the river.

Beside the elverers is an interested party, an old man, who has bargained for a couple of pounds from a catch for to-night's supper and to-morrow's breakfast. A good elver tide will empty the riverside pubs and leave the landlord fretting like a dog on his chain. The best way to cook elvers is to fry them in bacon fat; cooking turns them from grey to white, and on the table they look like spaghetti. They have a delicate flavour all their own, yet people eat so many of them during their short season that they see the last of them for the year without regrets. At the beginning of May elvers begin to turn black, owing to the formation of bone in the fish, and are thenceforth considered unfit to eat until they may be caught as eels.

There are a few of unsettled employment who make a seasonal profession of elvering. But perhaps the greatest devotee of the elver was the old man, who was determined to have 'all joy of the worm.' I think that he was one of those old tramps, who when their feet or their spirits give out, retire to live on Gloucester's western slope, where they earn shillings by gathering watercress, wild daffodils, mushrooms, blackberries, fungi, or whatever wild bounties the season affords. Either resolved never to miss an elver tide, or more likely to save himself the price of lodging, this old fellow went in a recent spring to Maisemore Bridge, where he lived, ate, and slept regardless of the weather. But mostly he slept, for when the elverers came out of the city they invariably found him dozing among his empty sacks, dreaming of the open road.

Sometimes an elver tide, full of promise, has a disappointing ebb at Maisemore if the flood-head sweeps the elvers past the weir. This happens when the tide is strong and the river is low, and an exceptionally dry February will see the elvers swept up to Tewkesbury on a mid-March tide, where normally the elver harvest is not expected until the powerful bore tides of April. Elvering is always better lower down or further up, and elvers are always more abundant elsewhere. Gloucester folk will speak of really large catches at Minsterworth, Epney, or Framilode. Framilode says elvering is better up at Minsterworth, and Minsterworth that the best elvering is up towards Tewkesbury. A village will sometimes have a large exportable surplus, which will be sold to a village that has not been so fortunate, and the price in recent years has varied from 1½d. to 1s. 6d. a pound. But away from the river nobody cares much about elvers, and in villages five miles away they will hardly find a buyer and, though they are sometimes sold in Cheltenham, they are the last to leave the fishmonger's slab. This is due to culinary ignorance, for on Severnside you will not only find the best eating but also the best cooking in England.

The upper end of Maisemore River is crossed by a weir, which the Bore approaches like a horse at a jump; the smaller bores refuse it, while the greater bores take it in their stride without slackening pace. In the month of May the salmon leap the weir on their journey up river, but he who would follow the salmon must leave the island by Maisemore Bridge. The present bridge is a temporary construction and several bridges have superseded the original, which was built

'In honore Dni nri Ihu Cristi qui nobis crucifixus erat.

Ceossie croz fist Willm fiz Anketill de Lilton, Et Ciseoli Willm
fiz Anketill comenza pont de Masemore.'

'For the honour of the Lord Jesus Christ, who was crucified for
us. William, son of Anketill of Lilton, made this cross, and the
same William son of Anketill began the bridge of Maisemore.'

It is to be hoped that William's bridge was not as shaky as
his Latin, which stumbles off into Norman-French, but his
words have a bold ring, proclaiming his faith in God and in
himself, for it was a brave undertaking to build a bridge over
the path of the Bore. It is significant that he began but
evidently was not spared to finish his work, and the present
builders of Maisemore Bridge might remember their predecessor
by incorporating his inscription in the structure of the new bridge.

A little above Over Bridge the river Leadon flows into
Maisemore River, leaving behind fields and woodlands, which
in March and early April are golden with wild daffodils.
England possesses no greater floral glory than these millions
of Lent lilies, which shine like stars in the Milky Way among
the favoured pastures of this valley. Wild flowers charm us
by their rarity, here they enchant us in their abundance.
The gipsies, encamped by Over Bridge, are great gatherers of
the wild daffodil which they hawk in the streets of Gloucester
and Cheltenham, and in the spring of 1944 a gipsy woman,
working on her own, took £9 in a day selling these wild flowers.

The Leadon curves round Lassington Hill to join the Severn.
On the summit of this hill, surrounded by woodland, stands
one of the great trees of England. The Lassington oak has a
girth of twenty-nine feet and was a sizable tree in the Middle
Ages, for it is estimated to be six hundred years old. It is
like a very old man walking on sticks, for it is propped up on
stout timbers; some of its great limbs have been amputated,
leaving stumps the girth of an ordinary full-grown oak. In
early summer this old giant proclaims his great age from afar,
for while his neighbours are in full leaf he is still a little thin
on top, as though the effort of putting forth leaves after so
many centuries was getting beyond his strength, yet in his
own slow time he flourishes in his full complement of foliage.

Once when the hunted fox had swum the river, the entire hunt clamoured to be ferried across. Thirty horses and their riders crowded on to the ferry, and it seemed to the ferryman that half the gentry of the neighbourhood were intent on committing suicide. For once the master of foxhounds was no longer general in the field; the ferryman was captain of his ship, he ordered the riders off the ferry, and ferried them in safety by relays. Some members of the hunt swam the river on their horses, but to this day the ferryman has a healthy contempt for the intelligence of foxhunters.

It is curious to see the Bore at Ashleworth. The wave, even on one of the great tides of the year, is never much more than three feet, yet when it has passed it is followed by another wave ten minutes later. This is caused through the Bore being broken by Alney Island, and the half that travels past Gloucester has two and a half miles further to go than the wave which sweeps up Maisemore River. Paradoxically, high water does not come to Ashleworth until the tide is well on the ebb. The tide runs up to Tewkesbury to swell like the back of a cat in anger against Tewkesbury Weir. The river at Ashleworth is still with the turn of the tide. Then, as this overfull reach of river hurries back to the sea, jostled by the natural and pent-up current of the stream, the water rises another six inches above the mark left by high tide. When this happens on a windless day you may see a considerable wave as the river current overtakes the ebbing tide.

Ashleworth is now a beef and dairy parish, and the great barn has become the finest and loftiest cow-shed in England. In the nearby village of Tirley the ritual of the corn-dolly was observed at harvest time. The dolly, no larger than a child's doll, the colour of walnut stain, looking like an African idol, may be seen in the Gloucester Folk Museum. It is roughly but cunningly made so that the joints of arms and legs move freely in sockets. At the end of the harvest, when the corn was carried, the last sheaf was left and the dolly dressed in its straw, before it was carried through the fields in thankfulness for what had been received and in propitiation for bounties to come. This custom has been and is still observed in varying forms by primitive peoples throughout the world, and the Tirley corn-dolly became a superstition long after it was an article of religion. How Herrick would have enjoyed the jollifications of the corn-dolly! The average Victorian parson would have viewed it with un-comfortable disapproval as a sign of pagan idolatry among his parishioners, and would have rejoiced in finding an opportunity for preaching a sermon on the subject of the second commandment at the harvest festival.

One can hardly see the revival of the corn-dolly in these days of tractor and binder. A country custom is borne on living tradition, and once that tradition has been broken from human memory with the death of a generation its revival is mere foolish pageantry. I once asked John Carter of Tirley, when he was seventy-six years old, whether he had any recollection of the corn-dolly, and he remarked: 'That must have been before I came to this country.'

John Carter is a man of genius. He is the village wheel-wright, who built the church clock entirely out of broken-down agricultural implements and machinery. Before I knew him and looked on his handiwork, I was prepared to meet some quizzical eccentric and be shown some fantastic parody of a clock's mechanism. He no longer works in the wheelwright's yard, but he is busy all day long in the workshop that lies under the thatched roof at the end of his cottage. He was at work in the inner recess when I disturbed him, and I was confronted by a lean old man looking like Michelangelo. His physical likeness to that painter's portrait is remarkable. I have looked on this picture many times, but had not seen it for nearly ten years when I met John Carter, yet the resemblance between him and the sixteenth-century painting was instantly recognizable. John Carter has the same deep-set, deep-seeing eye, the same high-boned, sunken cheek, the same wiry hair, his nose is smaller and unbroken but quite as aquiline, and though he is beardless, his moustache, close-clipped beneath the nose and trailing out around his sensitive mouth, completes the facial resemblance. Yet the most striking and extraordinary similarity is in the hands. Michelangelo's hand is one of the most memorable details in all painting; it might have been copied from John Carter's. I have never elsewhere seen such hands in living flesh; they are large hands with long fingers and knuckles of immense flexibility and power. They are hands made for the athletics of craftsmanship, and when they close on yours in the handclasp of greeting you know that you are touching no ordinary clay.

There are moments as I sit with John Carter in his workshop, surrounded by the materials of his active mind, when he reminds me of Don Quixote. This is partly due to his natural courtesy, which belongs to another age, and partly to the homely, commonplace things of the workshop, which throw the treasures of his personality into bolder relief. On the wall a pied blackbird, accidentally caught in a trap, hops like a miniature magpie in a cage. There are two very fine old brass clocks of such lovely tone that it is a pleasure to be here at the stroke of the hour, and enough musical instruments to set up several quartets and trios.

John Carter is an English villager living in the twentieth century, but his spirit belongs to the Renaissance. The extraordinary isolation of Severnside village life, surrounded by wide pastures, has allowed his mind to develop freely, within limits, and has prevented it from becoming overwhelmed by stereotyped modernity. I think that if he had been born elsewhere he would have made a great mark in the world. The son of a wheelwright, the yard soon claimed him in a district where wagons, gates, and all the gear of farming life made incessant demands upon his skill and toil. He could make a wheel out of raw tack, or build a wagon out of a beech-tree and a few rods of iron. But he was born with an interest in clocks and a love of music, gifts which he shared with his cousin, the late George Merrit, the blacksmith of Elmore.

John built the Tirley clock on the hundred-year-old lathe he inherited from his great-uncle, and no material from other clocks, or any part previously made for a clock, was used in its construction. A chaff-cutter, a roasting-jack, a bean-drill, a separator, a winnowing machine, a bicycle pedal, the brake rods of a cycle, a scythe, a cannon-ball, a pistol barrel, farmyard weights, crude, incongruous things were all used in building this delicate and accurate mechanism.

I have walked with old John from his cottage to the church on a Saturday afternoon, when he has gone to wind the clock. This he does regularly twice a week on Wednesdays and Saturdays. He is now very lame, having broken his leg close to the knee some years ago at the age of seventy, but with this infirmity he is far from decrepit, though he sets out from home with a stick and a crutch. He is also rather deaf and, because he is toothless, indistinct in his speech, but time has whetted his memory for the days that have been and he laments the decline that has overtaken Tirley.

'Now,' he says, 'we have nor a schoolmaster, nor a tailor, nor a cobbler, nor a coffin-maker, nor a gentleman, nor a lady in the village.'

He sometimes wonders why the church stands where it does and not 'up on the bank' (meaning 'up on the hill' in this part of the country), for the church and the house across the road are the only buildings in the village within the Severn's reach. In summer the river flows three-quarters of a mile away from here, but in winter floods lap round the churchyard. Though I looked across the great May flood of 1924, I never realized its depth, until John took me to the north-west corner of the church tower, where he had bored two holes and cut the word 'May'; it was a mere six inches below the great flood of 1852.

At one time Tirley church possessed a paddock, whose grass was reserved for church use, for the paddock was scythed in early summer and the fresh grass, laden with meadow flowers, strewed the church floor on Whit-Sunday. This custom persisted into the last century, but now even the exact where-abouts of this paddock are lost, and John tells me that it was 'dwindled and swindled away.'

The outside of the church is unremarkable, except for two

finely carved heads of a king and queen above the east
window. I imagined from the fine quality of their workman-
ship that they were old, but John told me: 'They were carved
by John Stafford of Staunton, an old workmate of mine. He
could use a mallet and chisel and bury a drop of beer, and
then stay teetotal for months.'

John has coffined many a body for this churchyard, where
his interest mingles with that jovial professional pride Shakespeare so well understood in those whose duty it is to cater
for and minister on death. 'There's two or three I've boxed
up there,' he explained, as his fine hand swept round the
subterranean extent of a vault.

The clock, whose face hangs rather low on the church
tower, was placed there as a memorial to Second-Lieutenant
George Edward Fowler, a Tirley farmer, killed near Ypres,
28th October 1917. One ascends to the workings of the clock
up a ladder and through a trap-door opened by a pulley,
another of John's inventions.

In the dim half-light of the church tower I felt that an
almost colourless painting by Rembrandt had come to life,
or that one of Leonardo da Vinci's mechanical and human
drawings had taken on the dimension of controlled movement.
Leonardo would have drawn the clock in faultless detail with
the same fidelity with which he would have drawn John
Carter's anatomy. Rembrandt would have loved the uncertain light of the tower, and would have left the clock in
ambiguity of shadow, contenting himself by painting the clock
in John Carter's face.

John lit a candle and moved the flame against the lettering,
which he had carved on the wooden base bed of the clock's
movement:

TIRLEY RAISED IN THIS TOWER OCT 31 1918
HUBERT JOHN CARTER MAKER WHEELWRIGHT & C.

The C at the end of this inscription stands not for clock-
maker, but carpenter. The clock has ticked through the
seconds and struck the hours for a quarter of a century, and

only the eye of a very great expert would be able to identify one or more of the origins in this movement. The wooden bed of the clock comes from the stout railings which John had erected in his youth at the side of Haw Bridge to prevent drunkards from falling into the Severn as they left the pub. With poetic significance the strike of the clock is lifted by the back of a scythe and the chime comes from a roasting-jack. These things of obsolescent usage blend with such prosaic things as the rods of bicycle brakes, which form the spindle of the clock. This is a period piece, representative of the great age of mechanical transition. Almost everything in the clock has some intimate association with the soil of Tirley parish.

It is fortunate that John Carter was born in a district where parochial poverty gave scope to his ingenuity, for having successfully built Tirley clock, eighteen years later he 'made Eldersfield' and, when it was dedicated by the bishop, 'They took over £5 in sixpences from people who came to see the clock.' On his work-bench is the skeleton of a third church clock, which John fears he may never complete, and I have not asked him if he has any tower in mind for its setting.

There is always something to engage his inventive skill. To amuse a child he has built a miniature windmill on top of a pole in his garden, which turns the legs and pedals of a doll on a bicycle. I think that he is happiest making musical instruments. Last winter he made two fiddles from old packing-cases, and the tone of some of the banjos he has made is hardly to be surpassed. He has also a fondness for flutes and clarinets, which he makes out of old cycle pumps, but now that he has few teeth he finds wind instruments easier to make than to play. It might seem facile to make a flute from a cycle pump, unless one has heard the purity of its notes.

In his workshop I picked up the neck of a bass viol he had carved, and imagined that he had set aside the work, for the wood was riddled with worm, but as John says: 'The older the tack the better the tune.' In his day John would play the cornet alongside any one, or the fiddle, the banjo, the guitar or the flute, but confesses that he 'never had no liking for the argon.'

John's grandmother was cook and dairymaid to Squire Hawkins of the Haw, the noble red-brick house beside the river. Squire Hawkins lived the life of a country gentleman of moderate means. He was a bachelor and needed to be, since few wives would have countenanced his robust habits. The squire had a pack of harehounds, and his country lay across the Severn in days before the bridge crossed the river close to his house. On winter mornings the squire began his day's hunting by riding from his front door into the river and swimming across to the meet, followed by his hounds. He would spend a glorious day chasing the hare over the level grounds between the Severn and Coombe Hill, a perfect hunting country with just enough water-jumps to add zest to the chase, and at the end of it a swim home.

'And when he died, they took him away and buried him in the Crypt Church at Gloucester,' said John regretfully, as though the parish had been cheated of his genial ghost.

The passing of such a gay bachelor as squire was a real loss to village life, for a squire who leaves an heir leaves an inheritance of local tradition, and village opinion sees that he lives up to it, or else 'he 's not the man his father was.'

Squire Hawkins was succeeded by Squire Baker. He too is still remembered. Sometimes in a Severnside inn on a morning when the frost has caught the early potatoes, or nipped the pear blossom, you may hear an old man say: 'I 've seen Squire Baker on his grey horse this morning.'

III. HIGH TIDE COMES TO TEWKESBURY

The Bore as it passes Tirley slumps, the wave disappears, but the tide continues to run. This dwindling of the wave is due to the tide running over greater depths of water, which have a tendency to absorb it, the Rye Pool above Haw Bridge being one of the deeper parts of the river. The Bore, however, is far from being spent; as it approaches Tewkesbury Lock it gushes with splendid force into the 'Old Severn.' This still backwater was once known as the Upper Lode, and was the main stream of the Severn, until the river was diverted to run over Tewkesbury Weir, when the lock was built in 1856. The tide as though guided by instinct seeks this old channel, which has become shallow through much mud, dredged from the river bed, being dumped here; and at times a string of barges, waiting to enter the lock, has been swung into the Old Severn by the force of the tide.

Time has stood still on the Old Severn, for nothing disturbs the placidity of its stagnant water except the arrival of the tide and the lazy splashings of occasional fish. The Old Severn curves for two hundred yards until it meets the ramp of earth above the lock which divides it from the current of the river. The tide breaks against this ramp before surging back in frustration to face the main stream. It dashes against the lock-gates and round the island, on which the lock-house stands, to quell the roar of the weir.

The highest Bores knock against the lock gates, which open up before them, and all four gates are on occasions thrown open by the force of the tide which continues to flow upstream. The weir, however, is only to be overcome when there is a considerable amount of fresh water flowing over it, raising the level of the river below the weir, thus reducing the height of the jump. The island dividing the lock from the weir is half covered in a plantation of persh, as the osier is called hereabouts. This ancient word gave the town of

18

Pershore its quaint and beautiful name, and the cuckoos, as they call incessantly in the spring among the persh at Tewkesbury Weir, recall the old local proverb, 'The cuckoo goes to Pershore fair, to buy a horse and ride away,' for Pershore fair was held at the end of June, but with the fair's decline the lovely cadence of this old saying has lost its significance though none of its charm.

At almost any time below the lock you will see kingfishers, though the river which sustains them at times almost brings about their extinction. A high flood in the nesting season, like that of May 1924, destroys the young birds. The two lock-keepers, who are keen observers of bird life, take an almost domestic interest in the birds which nest about the bank. A few seasons ago a sudden rise in the river sealed the hole of a kingfisher's nest, and the parent birds were seen pecking at the river bank in a vain endeavour to make another entry to their home. After two days the flood subsided and, to the lock-keepers' amazement, the young kingfishers had survived, for the nest in the bank had been above water. They had lived for two days without food, and, what was even more remarkable, they had apparently subsisted without any intake of fresh air. A greater tragedy than flood to the kingfishers are those rarer occasions when, in a severe winter, the river is frozen over. They are denied access to their natural food until the ice on the river is broken by passing traffic. They then dive into the water in their search for fish and, as often as not, rise to find themselves imprisoned under a layer of ice. Sometimes their plight has been noticed by the lock-keepers, who have broken the ice in an attempt to rescue them, but unfortunately they have never succeeded in saving one alive.

The kingfishers had for their nesting neighbours the sand-martins. The sand-martins, at great labour, build for themselves permanent nests to which they return every year. One winter during their absence the tide undermined their part of the river bank and, with their home from home destroyed, they left this part of the river to nest elsewhere. The only other riparian nest builder is the wren, who makes her nest in an old rat-hole. Bird visitors from the sea are few and irregular. They are the herring-gull, who is to be seen at all times of the year, the cormorant, and the common tern. A century ago—in 1845—an enormous flight of terns flew inland up the river as far as Worcester, and they were so thick that a number of them were killed by stones being thrown into their midst by astonished onlookers. This visitation coincided with the great shoals of sprats which entered the river and were so plentiful at Sharpness that they were caught by lowering buckets into the river, though it is hardly possible that any of these fish can have come as far as Tewkesbury.

The porpoise has been seen in this water, lured here no doubt by his appetite for the twait shad. In some years this fish has been so plentiful that the Upper Lode water has been alive with them. The last big year for twait was 1933 when fishermen filled their punts with them. The twait is the boniest of all fish and for this reason, though it has a pleasant enough flavour, is little esteemed locally. Some of the old fishermen had a knack of cutting this fish so that the bones easily came away from the flesh, but twait come in plenty at such irregular intervals that this art is now all but lost, and a man catching a few twait to-day contents himself with the roes and throws the rest of the fish away.

As crops are retarded by a late spring, so fish are held back by the temperature of the river. Even an elver has a mind of its own, and if a lot of snow-water from Wales is carried down river in late winter or early spring the elver horde will hardly venture up to Tewkesbury until towards the end of April. After mild winters they have 'tailed' their way over Tewkesbury Weir and have been caught in sizable quantities in the higher water. In April, too, the lampern is caught in the long conical basket known as a weel. But May is the month of the lamprey or 'stone-sucker,' who anchors himself to the stones of Tewkesbury Weir. He is still eaten and enjoyed by a few rivermen, but is more often cut up for eel-bait, since there is a prejudice against this fish, once so royally enjoyed, for many consider that a part of the lamprey is poisonous and local fishmongers rarely handle one. The lamprey gatherer is often rewarded by the sight of a salmon, who rises out of the depths of the river to leap the weir.

So strong is the salmon's instinct to jump that I have seen one throw himself against the side of a barge waiting to enter the lock, a jump which almost cost him his life. Before the lock was built vessels had often to wait a long time for flood or tide to carry them over the Upper Lode, and the craft of those days were as large as anything seen on the river to-day. Some of the barges and frigates were sixty feet long, single-masted with a square sail, and were capable of carrying sixty tons of merchandise. Before railway transport no one grudged waiting for the tide to have such cargoes carried upstream. Commonest of river vessels was the trow, an almost flat-bottomed sailing barge of up to as much as eighty tons displacement, which carried a fantastically large sail on a mast nearly eighty feet high. Such vessels would often have to wait at the Upper Lode, while the horse-drawn Betsy barges passed up river, for these barges were so built that they only drew three or four feet of water when loaded.

In times of flood vessels still pass over the weir, avoiding the lock. Any vessel laden at Bewdley passes free of toll through Tewkesbury Lock, for men of Bewdley fought for Edward IV at the battle of Tewkesbury, who rewarded their services by granting their town freedom of duties and tolls on the river Severn. This privilege, carelessly granted by an irresponsible king flushed with the success of victory, resulted in a minor civil war between Bewdley and her county city of Worcester. Three years after this concession had been granted the bailiffs of Worcester were claiming a penny from the owner of every Bewdley boat and fourpence a ton on all laden merchandise. Gloucester followed Worcester's example until an Act of 1503 was passed decreeing heavy penalties against any officer who prevented the passage of a Bewdley vessel, or demanded tolls of its owner. The two cities petitioned the Star Chamber against this Act, when the bailiffs

of Worcester plausibly suggested that if the city was deprived
of its tolls they might be unable to pay fee-farm of their city
due to the King's Highness. They extended their argument
by drawing attention to their bridge of stone, by which the
'kings subjects have their passage between Englond and
Walys,' and complained that boatmen with 'cordys and with
hokys and sparreys of yron drawith, hokyth, tyeith, and
puttyth at the said burgge and greytly fretyth, losyth and often-
times brekyth and castyth down the stones of the seyd burge,'
damage which the city of Worcester had to make good, and
the city claimed that it was entitled to charge for the use of
its towpath as its freehold.

Under these conditions Bewdley became a depot for goods
destined for Bristol and the south, while Worcester did her
best to make the Bewdley men's voyage as hazardous as
possible. Stones were thrown and even arrows shot as they
passed Worcester, in attempts to force them to land and pay
their tolls, or to sell their goods contrary to their intentions,
until in 1532 a further Act was passed imposing a penalty of
40s. on any one hindering passengers on the banks of the
Severn or demanding tolls of them. Tewkesbury, like Bewdley,
has had river troubles, for in the reign of Henry VI its bailiffs,
burgesses, and commonalty petitioned Parliament with a
complaint against the disorderly Forest of Dean men, who,
they said, come 'with great riot and strength, in manner of
war, as enemies of a strange country,' and stop and plunder
their barges of wheat, malt, and flour and other divers goods
'as they pass by the coasts near the forest and marauders
not only despoil them of their merchandise, but destroy their
vessels, and even cast the crews overboard and drown them.'

Tewkesbury has depended greatly on its river trade, and
shared with Gloucester the honour of providing the ship *Sutton*
to fight against the Spanish Armada. Yet within nine years
of this national crisis internal necessity resulted in a feud
between the two towns. This was a famine year in the vale
of Gloucester, wheat selling at 12s. 6d. a bushel at Tewkesbury,
and Gloucester placed a chain across her river to prevent food

TEWKESBURY ABBEY, SEVERN FLOOD

needed by herself being carried up river to Tewkesbury. This chain remained for several years until Tewkesbury petitioned the Privy Council, who ordered its removal. It would have been better for the town if the chain had remained for a few more years, for in 1604 Bristol trowmen brought plague to Tewkesbury, causing twenty-three deaths.

The river at summer level flows between high banks hidden from Tewkesbury's view, for the town is almost a mile away, yet a winter's flood brings the river up to the town's end, and in the great flood of 1770 the Severn flowed into the nave of Tewkesbury Abbey. Boats have on occasions been used in the town, and Tewkesbury has been entirely surrounded by water. The Avon, the Carrant, and the Swilgate have contributed to these floods, for, to quote an ancient writer: 'Tewkesbury, like the garden of Eden, is watered by four rivers.'

The rising ground between the Upper and Lower Lodes commands the finest view of the town and is unique among English landscapes. The Severn immediately below is nearly a hundred yards wide, and beyond it lies a mile of level pasture dominated by the great tower and nave of the abbey, whose cathedral-like size reduces the town to the insignificance of a village in relation to its parish church. An illusion which is most curiously enhanced by geography, for in the distance the Cotswolds rise to their greatest height of over one thousand feet, yet the great abbey is the keystone to this most fascinating optical illusion.

The Swilgate carries the highest tides up to the shadow of the abbey, where I have seen the narrow brook swollen by as much as two feet of water. Though the stream to-day would be considered barely navigable it played a large part in the building of the church, and without it this immense work might never have been undertaken.

There is a tradition, now hardly remembered, that stone from Caen was brought by sea, up the Severn and into the Swilgate for the building of the Norman abbey. The greater part of the building was carried out and completed by Robert, Earl of Gloucester, the illegitimate son of Henry I, who was born at Caen. Robert had a great love for his native town, and he certainly had Caen stone shipped to Bristol for the building of his castle, and gave some of this stone for the building of Saint Augustine's Priory. It is probable, therefore, that part at least of Tewkesbury Abbey is Norman in more than style, and that some of its stone is Norman in origin. Indeed, in the twelfth century it may have been easier to bring stone by water from Normandy than to carry it across country, a dozen miles or so, from the Cotswolds to Tewkesbury.

The abbey has seen most of Tewkesbury's history, the burials of its lords and the marriages of its ladies, in the complicated and forgotten plots of medieval power politics.

Even the final blows of the battle of Tewkesbury were delivered under its roof when in the rout the Yorkists pursued the beaten Lancastrians into the nave, where many were cut down and others were dragged from sanctuary and murdered.

The great building still stands to the abiding glory of the town, through the loyalty of the people of Tewkesbury for their church, at the time of the suppression of the monastery, when they paid Henry VIII the sum of £483 for its ransom.

A little above the weir the Avon joins the Severn, and it is near here that Theoc, the Northumbrian hermit, who gave his name to Tewkesbury, had his cell early in the eighth century.

In character the two rivers are wholly dissimilar, for though an excess of Severn tide sometimes flows into the Avon's mouth, the Avon is essentially a midland river and neither the salmon nor the elver ventures up its stream. Yet at one time, before long-net fishing was prohibited above the weir, large quantities of salmon were taken from Barge Pool just below the confluence. Indeed, salmon were once so plentiful at Tewkesbury, that parents who apprenticed their sons in the town stipulated that they should not be fed on salmon more than twice a week. Nowadays a salmon is hardly to be taken legally in Tewkesbury water.

The river was unbridged between Gloucester and Worcester until Thomas Telford, in 1826, crossed it at the Mythe, Tewkesbury, with a single span. As a preliminary to the

Mythe Bridge the capital sum of £1,650 was paid for the rights of the Upper Lode ferry, which crossed the now stagnant water of the Old Severn. Telford was nearly seventy when he came to Tewkesbury and, with a lifetime of experience as a bridge-builder, he under-estimated the cost of the Mythe Bridge at £20,700. The bridge cost £35,000, but Telford was saved financial embarrassment by the neighbourly help of Thomas Taylor of the Mythe, who advanced him £16,000 to complete his work. The bridge is a graceful structure, and a fine example of the dawn of the second Iron Age. It also bears witness to the artistic nature of an engineer of genius, for Telford, despite his tremendous preoccupations as a bridge-builder and canal-maker, was a great reader of poetry and a writer of verse. Among his mighty achievements he linked the Baltic with the North Sea by means of the Gotha canal, crossing Sweden from Stockholm to Gothenburg. But the Severn is indissolubly associated with this great man's name, for it was a few years after completing the Mythe that Telford again bridged the Severn on Maisemore River at Over.

The beautiful red cliff of the Mythe descends to the water's edge, and its red soil has the distinction of being almost the last spot in England to nourish the woad plant in its natural state. It is extraordinary that woad, once so extensively used by the ancient Britons, should now be almost extinct in Britain. Pliny the elder writes, that 'matrons and girls among the Britons stain the body over when taking part in the per-formance of certain sacred rites, and rivalling the dusky Ethiopians they go naked.' Woad, however, continued to be cultivated as a mordant or base for dyes, and as much as £20 a ton was paid for the best woad. Queen Elizabeth I when shown the woad used by the Gloucester dyers was not amused, for she ordered that no more of that 'eville smellinge plant should be sown.' The thought of woad next her skin was too much for the queen. Woad probably found its way to the Mythe from a root or seeds from a barge laden with the weed on its way to Gloucester, and the cliff's red face of bare earth gave the plant an opportunity for cultivating itself.

The Severn is reputed to be the boundary of the nightingale's song, but every May the nightingales are in splendid voice on the Mythe, rising exultantly above the songs of other birds. One morning I stood here listening to the nightingale, the thrush, the blackbird, the linnet, and the ubiquitous cuckoo, when suddenly an unseen woodpecker began tapping a tree. Beethoven could not have introduced the drum more skilfully into a symphony.

The oddest bird visitor to this part of the river is the cormorant, who, common enough on the lower Severn below Gloucester, has recently made excursions far inland. And great was my surprise and pleasure to see the head and neck of a cormorant swimming three hundred yards above the Mythe Bridge. This bird gives an almost tropical splendour to the Severn for those who know the great rivers of Africa, for there is no more conspicuous bird on the Zambesi, the Congo, and the Upper Nile than the ibis, and, although dissimilar enough to the ornithologist, a cormorant in the water is very like an ibis. Their heads and necks are alike, and they share the same habit of diving and reappearing without any warning.

I watched this cormorant dive and then conjectured where he would reappear. I waited a minute and my guess was wide by fifty yards. He was swimming towards me, and he was not alone for his mate was with him. I walked along the river bank to meet them and found that during one of their long dives they had passed me. Their passage upstream was spasmodic as they veered aimlessly now one side, now the other of the river, yet despite this and the flow of the stream they were making as much progress as I on my two legs along the river bank. I was prepared to follow them as far inland as their fancy might take them, but the birds as though sensing my intention took wing. There are few birds more spectacular in flight than a cormorant as he rises from the water. With only his head and long neck showing above water he launches himself on the air. His small head and thin neck gives no indication of his great size, for he is among the largest of

MYTHE BRIDGE

British birds. With the exception of the swan, only the gannet and the heron have a greater length of body, and they only exceed the cormorant's three feet by an inch; he is as large as a golden eagle.

As these great birds rose from the river they looked as fantastic as witches riding on broomsticks against this background of inland scenery. I would have expected them to take a short cut over pasture on their flight towards the Upper Lode, but they carefully followed the channel of the stream, so that one could have mapped the course of the river in the sky until they were out of sight.

Several large ponds lie inside the river bank beyond the Mythe, known as the claypits; for the bricks that gave medieval and Tudor Tewkesbury its Georgian façade were made here. With some of the remaining bricks several cottages were built on the ramp of earth dividing the pits from the river, osiers were planted, and families made a living by making pott-hampers for fruit. Most winters, and sometimes during an exceptionally rainy summer, these houses are visited by flood, which compels families to live upstairs for an indefinite period and then to scour the river mud out of the kitchen and living-room after the flood has gone. Only a real Severnsider, who has enjoyed these emergencies in childhood and has been spared going to school for a week or two in consequence, can face these discomforts with detachment and philosophy. Such a one is Arthur Payne, who lives by himself in the last house.

Any one meeting Arthur for the first time would be struck by his fine blue eyes, which are remarkably clear for a man of his years. And although his eyes are perfectly matched, he has been blind in one of them since birth, yet he is an amazing marksman, and, what is more extraordinary, his favourite weapon is the catapult, which he learnt to use as a boy. I have seen him hit the trunk of a tree from across the Severn where the river is seventy-two yards wide, and rats, rabbits, and hares frequently fall victims to his skill. He has shot as many as a dozen rabbits in an afternoon with his catapult, though he never aims at a bird, unless it is to scare the swan feeding on his ground-bait in the claypits, and a hit at fifty yards is a mere pin-prick to a swan.

Arthur has a great affection for the corncrake, since it was a hobby of his to call the crake. This he did by means of a 'caller' and he showed me the extraordinary instrument he used for this purpose. A caller has a wooden cog, some two inches in diameter, which runs in the slotted end of a wooden handle. A thin wooden lath is nailed to the end of the handle with its loose end pressing against the end of the cog. When the free side of the cog is run against the trouser leg, it rasps the lath with the sound of crake, crake, crake. The monotonous note of the corncrake is perfectly reproduced and the running of the cog enables it to be repeated with the tireless call of the bird. It is an exact and hideous repetition of the most strident bird-call in our land, and it even deceives the bird himself. A boy with this ingenious toy will hide himself behind a bush to play his practical joke on this shy bird in the mating season. He runs the caller down the side of his breeches and watches the corncrake's reply to the simu-lated call of love, as the bird runs towards the rasping refrain of the caller.

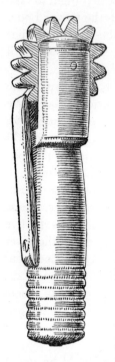

Arthur has succeeded in bringing the love-lorn corncrake to within a few feet of his caller, until the bird, aware of the trick that had been played on him, has flown off with a flight like that of the moorhen, whom he so much resembles. The moorhen though small makes an excellent meal, being only a little inferior to the partridge in flavour. Arthur tells me that many people make the mistake of skinning the bird, and thereby rob the carcass of its rich natural fat, which is not to be artificially replaced in cooking. The bird is, however, a difficult one to pluck unless first scalded in boiling water. The fox appreciates moorhen meat, for one morning Arthur surprised a fox swimming in the claypits in pursuit of three moorhens. The birds escaped when the fox got wind of Arthur.

The view from here is a variation of the loveliest in the midlands with the Malvern hills:

> Fashioned so carelessly to lovely shapes
> To please the eye,
> Then steeped in dye of grapes . . .
> But do not think that I this beauty caught
> In my bold eye.
> These ancient hills in sunlight and in shade
> First taught me with a cloud's caress
> A knowledge of earth's loveliness.

They are, indeed, geologically speaking, about the oldest thing in England to which man has given a name. These pointed hills which rise so steeply from the Severn plain have the grandeur of mountains, as their majestic blueness, in contrast with the greens of Bredon and Cotswold, lowers with the strangeness of a foreign land. They gave birth to the rugged utterance of *Piers Plowman* and they excited Byron, who as a boy saw them from Cheltenham, before he dreamed of Greece.

These hills dominate the Severn from Tewkesbury to Worcester. When the tide appears on these reaches it is spoken of locally as a quarrage, for it is not a sea-tide, but is brought about by the pressure of sea-tide against the fresh water, and, despite Tewkesbury Weir, fourteen inches of quarrage have been recorded against Diglis Lock below Worcester.

The quarrage is rare, unpredictable, with little or no influence upon the natural life of the river, and its arrival, though a thing of wonder, is more a matter of academic than of general interest.

IV. DEERHURST AND THE LONG-NET

The Saxon buildings of Deerhurst, though of interest to the archaeologist, are best understood in terms of geology, for after nearly nine hundred years they look incongruous in their setting, where they stand close to the river bank without neighbouring architectural affinity. The stones of Odda's chapel and Deerhurst church were brought here from the shores of the Severn near Westbury, and were gathered from the slabs of lias, many of which still remain, at the foot of the eastern end of Garden Cliff.

The stone was quarried by nature and its naturally smooth slabs gave little trouble to the builder. To any one coming to Deerhurst, fresh from the controlled architectural power of Tewkesbury's Norman abbey, the church for all its interest seems lacking in style and fulfilment. Though the two churches belong to two different epochs, their respective achievements are divided by only a lifetime. Deerhurst represents the culmination of Saxon architecture, for the church was built by Edward the Confessor and was completed ten years before the Conquest, when the pious king refounded the priory that the Danes had sacked half a century earlier.

Odda's chapel, eighty yards away, is of the same date. In its day it was considered a great building, for a votive tablet in Latin describes it as a royal palace dedicated to the Holy Trinity, yet it is so insignificant that after the Reformation it became the dairy to the adjoining half-timbered farmhouse. A Deerhurst villager has told me that his father ate his meals in this building, before archaeologists discovered its antiquity and significance. Though a visit to Deerhurst is an experience for the antiquarian, to the historian it serves as a reminder of the poverty of Saxon civilization.

A natural asset may have been responsible for the early foundation of Deerhurst, for at one time a small island lay in the middle of the Severn a little below Deerhurst church. At this point the river must have been easily fordable, since barges were often prevented from passing here for want of water. The island was known as Deerhurst Tail, and the bargees who grounded here must on occasions have had to wait a fortnight for the tide to carry them past this spot. Throughout the ages villagers have had little love for rough, river-going men, but, grounded on Deerhurst Tail, the bargees, with a peculiarly English sense of humour, held their wakes on this little island in imitation of the village midsummer revels, for naturally only in summer months, when the river was especially low, were they so becalmed. Owing to floods, the constant impact of the river, and the navigation weirs at Gloucester, Deerhurst Tail has completely disappeared; vanished too is the rough hilarity which inspired these wakes. You may look on the unbroken water of this reach of the Severn, and then remember the bargees who once did high satyric festival in the middle of the river.

On this spot, as recently as 1933, a seal was seen in the river, where he remained for some time to the embarrassment of local bathing belles who refused to share the river with him. What happened to the harmless fellow I have never been able to discover, so possibly aided by the stream he made his way back to the sea. Deerhurst is a parish of strange fauna, where as a small boy I had my first view of the Severn and was delighted to find most of the hutch varieties of rabbit running wild with the rabbits of the field among the meadows. It was soon after the end of the 1914–18 war, and these rabbits, which had been assiduously bred in hutches, had been turned loose to breed with the wild rabbits with a view of improving the weight of the latter. There were white rabbits, black rabbits, black-and-white rabbits, and white-and-brown rabbits. I doubt if they ever crossed or transgressed with the wild rabbit, which was plentiful enough hereabouts, for the wild rabbit must have been contemptuous of the tame rabbit and, though they ran together, I think that the wild rabbit was suspicious of a kindred creature released from captivity. The tame breeds were an easy mark for their natural enemies, the fox and stoat, and completely disappeared after a few generations.

On this my first visit to the river I was alone, and I caught my first and only live Severn salmon. It was only a pink, a little less than three inches long, but I was only eleven. I had been allowed to go home after spending the first hour of the three hours' service on Good Friday in Tewkesbury Abbey; instead I wandered down to the Severn and on to Deerhurst. I realize now that because it was Good Friday the Bore, which usually runs that day on account of the proximity of the Easter moon, reached Tewkesbury that morning. It swept my salmon into one of those miniature lagoons the cattle puddle with their feet by the river's edge when they go down to water, for here my salmon swam in landlocked solitude. After some skirmishing I captured him in my hands; he was the exact miniature replica of a salmon as seen on a fishmonger's slab. I took him home and, it being Good Friday, announced that I would eat him with my tea. But at home no one would believe my assertion that this was a salmon, and I was denied the child's mouthful he might have made. Familiarity with the river has often reminded me that in truth he was a salmon, if only a pink. To this small fish I owe my first intimacy with the river, and a sense of expectancy of meeting with the unfamiliar along the Severn's path and shore ever since.

The houses clustered about the church give the impression that Deerhurst is a small village. It is in fact a large parish, covering the whole of the ancient hundred of Deerhurst, which became the endowment of the priory. Sir Robert Atkyns in *The Ancient and Present State of Gloucestershire*, a work which he wrote in the reign of Queen Anne, tells the extraordinary story how 'a serpent of prodigious bigness was a great grievance to all the country about Deerhurst, by poisoning inhabitants and killing their cattle. The inhabitants petitioned the king and a proclamation was issued out, that whosoever should kill the serpent should enjoy an estate on Walton Hill, which then belonged to the Crown. One John

PEAR BLOSSOM AT ELMORE

Smith, a labourer, undertook it and succeeded, for finding the serpent lying in the sun, with his scales ruffled up, he struck between the scales with his axe and struck off his head. The family of the Smiths enjoy the estate at present; and Mr. Lane who married a widow of that family has the axe in his possession.'

This story, though it sounds incredible, is undoubtedly true; Sir Robert, a gentleman of the county and a member of Parliament, would hardly have had his intelligence ridiculed by country yeomen. Deerhurst became Crown property with the dissolution of the monasteries in the reign of Henry VIII, and it was most likely he or Edward VI who offered the reward. This event, therefore, probably took place between 1536 and 1553. If it had occurred in the reigns of Mary or Elizabeth, the word queen would have been substituted for king, and had it been either of the first two Stuart kings, Atkyns would have almost certainly have mentioned it as he was born in the reign of Charles I.

This quaint story probably became the basis of so many fairy-tales that the original came into disrepute, just as Dick Whittington, who was born across the Severn only a few miles from here, has become the theme of countless pantomimes. The serpent most likely came from South America, or the mainland or isles of the Caribbean, in a shipment of merchandise, and remained undetected while bargemen and trowmen were holding one of their wakes on Deerhurst Tail.

There are still a number of Smiths in Deerhurst, as in every village in this land. One of them was buried in Deerhurst churchyard in 1940 at the age of one hundred and two. I once asked Alfred Smith of Severnside, Apperley, about John Smith of Walton Hill, but he had never heard of the story and seemed uninterested in so incredible a tale, which surprised and disappointed me, for Alfred is keenly interested in the past.

Life has continued with medieval simplicity into Alfred's days. He remembers his grandmother using flint and tinder for want of matches, old corduroy trousers being specially

* B

treasured as tinder. In those days Severnside was amazingly self-sufficient. Alfred's father farmed in the old Saxon way; he dug seven-yard plots along the river bank on either side of the claypits with a spade, and sowed corn to provide bread for his family of ten children. This small crop ripened just as the salmon season ended, and the harvest, cut with sickles, was threshed by a friendly farmer. The corn was rowed up-river to Tewkesbury, where the miller ground it to flour, in which state it was returned to Apperley where it was baked in the home oven. Alfred used to go with the barm-can to fetch the yeast from the brewery in Tewkesbury.

Even the river provided this household with its coal, which was dredged from the river bed—a practice which continued until the 1880s, when it had been carried on for at least a century, for Samuel Rudder, writing prior to 1770, describes this operation:

'They sink a net with its mouth extended by an iron hoop of a semicircular form and a person stirs the river with a long pole just before the net, by which means and by the assistance of the current the coals roll into it. Five or six boats are sometimes employed in this business at a time.'

It seems unlikely that this coal was an outcrop; it was almost certainly jetsam from passing barges, for bargees, ever dishonest, frequently lightened their cargoes when forced to navigate the river shallows, one of which occurred at Haw Bridge. When the river was at low summer level, the river-men of Apperley, Chaceley, and Tirley must have watched many a hundredweight thrown overboard, which was destined to keep them warm through the winter. The building of the navigation weirs at Maisemore and Llanthony, giving as it did a greater depth of water to this reach of river, removed the temptation to throw coals overboard hereabouts, and with it died the profitable pastime of fishing for coal.

Indeed, along this part of the river folk expected all their fuel for nothing, for Rudder complains that all the way to Tewkesbury 'tenants have lopped almost every oak.' This was presumably done surreptitiously, since by ancient right they were entitled to lop from timber damaged by storm. 'An unpardonable injury in this part where coal comes cheaply down the Severn.' This custom has since died out and the oaks have recovered from their wounds. But the cheapness of coal, thanks to easy river transport, made the practice of river dredging all the more extraordinary, since Staffordshire coal has been delivered along this river bank as cheaply as 11s. a ton within living memory.

I have been surprised at a sharp hint of bitterness in his voice when Alfred has spoken of the enclosure of the common fields, for I had imagined that the memory of this great wrong had vanished from the rural mind, since most of this part of England was enclosed in the latter half of the eighteenth century. However, a large common extended from Deerhurst for several miles along the river as far as the parish of Leigh, and remained unenclosed long after other common land had been reft from the peasantry and divided into farms. This common enabled a family like the Smiths to prosper in complete social and economic independence until, as an afterthought to a great wrong inflicted by the will of the minority against the interests of the majority, the land was enclosed, without compensation to the families who for generations had enjoyed its communal benefits.

The enclosures came with the rotation of crops, the improvement of stock, and better methods of farming. They forced the peasantry, who had benefited from the common fields, to plough and sow, hedge and ditch the land which had been stolen from their common heritage in return for a pittance that kept them and their families just above the borderline of starvation. They made possible the industrial revolution by driving thousands through rural want to the cities in the vain hope that an extra shilling or two a week would earn for them a fuller and richer life. The enclosures suppressed a deep, abiding instinct in the inarticulate heart of the English countryman, and forced him to find consolation and appeasement to his spirit in the unenclosed lands of distant continents,

But here on Severnside, thanks to the bounty of the river, something of the old independence of the peasantry still persists, and the river with its recurrent floods probably preserved Deerhurst Common from being enclosed until a later date.

Alfred has a theory that Severn floods were less severe in olden times than they are nowadays. He rightly contends that Deerhurst was once heavily forested and the wild boar was chased through the forest in the days of King John. Memorials of this ancient forest are to be seen in the few remaining great oaks still standing within a dozen yards of Severn bank.

'Now,' Alfred argues, 'a forest cannot grow on boggy ground, and least of all will the oak flourish there'; for this reason, he says, 'floods were not what they are to-day. Our flood-water comes from Wales, and improved drainage has turned Welsh bogs and marshes into Severn floods, for when the Welsh valley of the Severn was a marsh, the sun had time to suck up the moisture. To-day it hurries down to the sea.'

Against this interesting theory there is historical evidence of floods far exceeding the highest within living memory. The flood of 1770 reached the upper storeys of low-lying houses in Deerhurst. The chronicler Holinshed has described the flood of 1484 when many men, women and children, cattle and sheep were drowned by flood at Tewkesbury; 'several persons were drowned in their beds, children in cradles swam about the fields, and beasts were drowned even on the hills.' A century later, in Shakespeare's day, it was still called the 'great water' or 'Buckingham's water,' as it prevented Buckingham from crossing the Severn with the Welsh forces who had risen against Richard III.

This flood was probably the greatest ever experienced along this part of the river, yet a normal flood, when the Severn tops and overflows its banks, covers the land anything up to a mile on either side of the river between Tewkesbury and Gloucester. There are few winters that escape such visitations, and from time to time summer floods may, with unpredictable suddenness, drown the land and endow the scenery with fantastic beauty.

Such floods have prevented the nobility and landed gentry from building their homes along the river bank. Indeed the only country house along this part of the river, and that a modest one, is the Haw. Its situation was no doubt responsible for Squire Hawkins remaining a bachelor, for what lady would share a home with a man where any week in the year she might see her furniture floating around the parlour, her carpets spoiled, and a sediment of mud thick enough to raise a crop of radishes left indoors by the receding flood?

The villager is careful to live away from the flood lands, and though the churches of Deerhurst and Ashleworth lie near to the river, the houses that stand about them are little more than hamlets, separated from the main part of the village. The man who dwells on the river bank lives there because the river is his livelihood, where he enjoys an almost gipsy-like existence, independent of the intimate community of village life. His true affinities are along the river. He is a picker-up of unconsidered trifles. He will poach rabbits from his boat when they have sought refuge along the hedgerows from the flood. He will on rare occasions shoot the otter, and thereby rid the river of an enemy of the salmon and provide himself with a skin which may be marketed for as much money as a man may earn in a week. His hunter's eye is ever on the alert for visiting birds; at the right time of the year mallard and wild goose are frequently to be seen, and sometimes the only evidence of the rarer visitors to the river is the news that they have fallen to the wild-fowler's gun.

Alfred Smith has shot the great northern diver at Apperley, but he prefers bringing down a goosander, for he gets five and a tanner a time for a goosander in Tewkesbury. With fifty years' experience as a salmon fisherman he has twice caught sturgeon at Apperley. Alfred began fishing as his father's assistant at the age of eleven, and it was during his third season that a sturgeon came pounding into the long-net near the river bank. They grounded his head, which was secured by Alfred's father sitting on the fish, while Alfred did what he could with the tail. A cord was run through the fish's gills, and father and son set out to tow the fish home. In this position the fish almost took command of the Smiths' boat, which he swung round in circles, till after a long tussle they got him home and finally sent him to the fishmonger in Tewkesbury.

The long-net is one of the four legitimate methods of catching a salmon along the tidal Severn, and is the only method which can be employed upon the deep-water reaches of the river between Tewkesbury and Minsterworth. Long-net fishing, once the principal occupation along this stretch of river, has fallen into decline, though this ancient craft is still maintained by a few veterans.

The net has to be made to fit the river, and the net used at Apperley needs to be ninety yards long and twelve feet deep. This is not a simple matter of netting, for the net is shaped so that it swells in the centre into the 'swill,' a bulge, which is the opening to the cod, a great tapering bag in the net like the foot of a sock. The word cod gives a hint of the great antiquity of the long-net, for it probably derives from the Anglo-Saxon word *codd*, meaning a small bag, or may possibly get its name from the cod-pieces worn by medieval dandies.

Fishermen who talk of knitting their nets use the right expression, for the shaping of swill and cod has to be made with as much care as the foot of a stocking on a gigantic scale. It takes an experienced hand two months to knit one of these nets and a net will last only one season, so knitting must begin before the storms of winter have winnowed the last autumnal leaves from the oak if the net is to be ready for the opening of the season on 2nd February. Nets are made in the limited space of riverside cottages, and when outhouse and downstairs are flooded knitting is carried on in the bedrooms, where fishermen work untiringly through long winter evenings at the net on which the success of the coming season depends. In the last week of January the fishermen, for it takes a team of four to work a long-net, sweep the river.

A long-net is worked over a quarter of a mile of water; here the bed of the river is dragged with a heavy chain to remove all waterlogged timber and the roots of trees, which have become lodged there in the course of winter floods. Some of the timbers, rolled here by the current of the river, weigh many hundredweight and would tear the bottom out of a net if it became entangled on one of their spurs.

On 2nd February the long-net is placed in the river for the first time; it is paid out from a flat-bottomed punt, being weighted to the bottom of the river by a series of leads and buoyed to the surface by a number of corks. The line of corks runs diagonally across the surface of the river to prevent the cod from being turned inside out by the force of the current. The net is controlled from either bank by two bridles, one fastened to the bottom, the other to the top of each side of the net. The net, slanting in a crescent across the river, places the bridles on the Apperley bank further downstream than those on the Chaceley bank across the river. Thus the Apperley side of the net has to take the greater strain; for this reason these bridles are longer and are held together by a long line known as the muntle. In this position the muntle line is hauled over a quarter of a mile down the river bank with the current, while those holding the opposite bridles keep pace on the Chaceley side of the water. In motion the swill swells, the cod becomes rigid, and there is little hope for the oncoming fish. Upwards, ever upwards, is the one instinct of the salmon ascending towards his spawning grounds. The tapering swill and narrower cod make him think that he will get through this obstacle. A very strong fish sometimes breaks through a net, but apart from this he has little chance of getting away if he happens to be in a reach of river where a long-net is in operation. In this part of the river salmon swim deeply and in the opaque water are invisible to the eye. When the long-net has been drawn over its appointed quarter of a mile, the muntle is carried across the river, where a windlass draws the net into a horseshoe against the bank. In this position the current carries the cod downstream as far as a stage, which has been built for the purpose of landing the net. This stage is called the flake and differs from an ordinary river landing-stage, for its timbers, instead of running at right angles to the stream, are parallel to the river so as to give purchase to the fishermen's feet when landing the net. The cod with its catch is pulled to the flake and up the bank, where the fish are killed with a knobbler, a fifteen-inch wooden truncheon, made whenever possible of laburnum wood on account of its exceptional hardness.

Three or four salmon in the cod are here considered an excellent haul, though below Gloucester catches tend to be more plentiful, and one old cowman at Longney assures me that in his young days he assisted in a drag when twenty-one salmon were landed. The great enemy of long-net fishing above Gloucester is the increase of barge traffic; horse-drawn barges were content to wait while fishermen finished their drag. The motor-barge gives warning of its coming and, unless nearing the end of their drag, fishermen are expected to make way for its passage. The motor-barge pollutes the river to the detriment of salmon, and fish are often mutilated through being cut by passing propellers.

But the greatest deterrent to long-net fishing and salmon fishing generally, along the length of tidal Severn, has been the cost of a licence. The riverman will give ungrudgingly of his skill and labour to knit a long-net, but resents having to pay £10 for the privilege of working the long-net for a short season between February and August. The countryman is not a gambler, and the riverside peasant with little or no working capital resents throwing £10 in the river for doubtful returns. This sum would keep him and his family for a month, and 'a bird in the hand is worth two in the bush.' The short-sighted policy of high licences, despite the possible returns of a good season's fishing, has done much to diminish a time-honoured occupation in which chance plays so large a part. There is a real danger that the craft of making and the skill of using the long-net, together with the use of the lave-net in the lower reaches of the river, will vanish from Severnside

before the end of the century. Such skilled and useful occupations belong to the varied fabric of our national life and as
such should be encouraged to persist.

Long-net fishermen have at times to face an adverse season.
Alfred Smith and three others worked the long-net at Apperley
every day for seven weeks, a quarter of the entire season,
without catching a fish. In addition to the licence bringing
no return, the net during these seven weeks was wearing out,
'for your water is a sore decayer' of salmon nets. A net is
tarred at the opening of the season and again after three
months' use. To the inexperienced eye the net in August
might seem good for another season's fishing, but the salmon
is a strong swimmer and has even been known to break a new
net. From this it will be seen that once the continuity of
knitting a fresh net every winter is broken, the skill and
practice of making the long-net may be lost for ever.

In a good salmon season at Apperley more fish have been
caught than the local market has been able to absorb, and
they have an ingenious method of keeping salmon alive for a
week or ten days, until such time as the market for salmon
will be freer. These fish are stored in a 'trunk'; this is an
ordinary flat-bottomed Severn punt, eighteen inches deep, in
which a central chamber or hold has been portioned off and
filled with water from holes in the side. Here the salmon
live like prisoners in their river dungeon, while awaiting
execution by the knobbler. Of all Severn fishermen Apperley men are the most skilled in keeping caught fish alive;
their cunning is probably a heritage from the old days when
their ancestors were minions to the whims and appetites of
the petulant lords of Tewkesbury.

Alfred's second sturgeon, which was taken in the long-net,
was kept alive by this means, coffined for several days in a
punt entirely filled with water. In this imprisoned fashion
he was seen by a number of Gloucester folk, who interrupted
their steamer trips up river to pay 6d. a time for a peep at
the royal fish. Indeed, more was made by showing the fish
than the £2 that the fishmonger ultimately paid for this

sturgeon. The salmon is the money-making fish of the
Severn and more would have been got for a good-sized salmon
than for this sturgeon. The once esteemed lamprey from
time to time comes into the long-net and fishermen find them
difficult to market at 1s. 6d. a time, though in the thirteenth
century, to check profiteering, Henry III forbade any Severn
lampreys to be sold for more than 2s. each, and these were to
be sold to the sheriff for the royal kitchens. To-day the
lamprey is cut up as eel-bait, for the eel is relished above all
fish on Severnside.

There are at least five different ways of catching Severn
eels. One of them is similar to the long-net method of
catching salmon. The habits of the eel are in almost every
respect opposite to those of the salmon, except that both fish
live part of their lives in the ocean and part in the river.
But while the salmon grows in the sea and spawns in the
river, the eel fattens in the river and spawns in the sea.
Some six or eight weeks elapse between the end of the salmon
season and the short zenith of the eel harvest, when the eel
relies on the river current, swollen by autumnal rain, to carry
him seawards. A Severn eel-net is in principle similar to a
salmon long-net, except that the cod below the open swill
drifts away into a ten-foot alley ten inches wide, which is
kept taut under water by a series of hoops. The largest of
these eel-nets is fifty feet long with a three-inch mesh
diminishing towards the cod, and, owing to the propensity
of eels to move near the bed of the river, the net is eighteen
to twenty feet in depth.

A full-sized net, because of its finer mesh, takes three months
to knit and is immensely heavy, yet an eel-net will last a
fisherman twenty seasons, for the migration of eels, passing
down river at the rate of nine and a half miles a day, allows
for little more than seven or eight nights in the year in which
eels may be caught by this method. Unlike the long-net,
the eel-net is not dragged downstream, but is moored with its
swill facing the current, and two-and-a-half-inch ropes and
chains are needed to secure the bridles of these nets to the

trunks of long-established trees. Even then the force of the
river sometimes breaks the mooring, causing the net to snap
back to the bank at the cost of a night's fishing.

The cod of an eel-net is detached from the swill, enabling
the catch to be secured, and sometimes as much as two
hundredweight is taken in a haul. This is the only method
whereby eels may be taken in any commercial quantity from
the Severn. The most favoured place for this type of fishing
is on the Llanthony Severn, just below Gloucester, for here
the channel is narrow and the river uninterrupted by passing
traffic, which is a most serious menace to this type of static
fishing.

Alfred Smith has the finest collection of eel-nets in existence,
for he has knit nets to fit the Severn, the Swilgate, the Chelt,
the canal, and smaller nets for some of the Chaceley brooks
and watercourses. He takes great care of these nets, which
are slung from the ceiling of his outhouse to keep them out of
flood's way.

A homelier and more usual method of catching eels for the
cottage table is with the putcheon or weel. This is a long
wicker basket, shaped like the straw covering of a wine bottle,
being some three feet long and baited at its end with a piece
of lamprey or rabbit. The weel lies on its side, anchored to
a stone on the bed of the river near the bank. The eel slides
easily into such a trap and would as easily slide out again
were it not for a cunning valve, the chale, a wicker cone,
like a dome within a dome. The eel slips through the small
hole at the end of the chale into the weel, and, if he has a
mind to return the way he came, is confused, for instead of
finding a smooth alley of wicker-work, he meets a palisade of
rough points at the end of the chale. Some putcheons and
weels have a double chale, a second chale being higher up
the putcheon to make escape for the eel almost impossible,
for he has reached his bait to find himself imprisoned in
a maze.

The word putcheon is used very loosely on Severn for any
basket-fishing, but round Gloucester a putcheon is the smallest

V. SQUIRE HAWKINS'S COUNTRY

A comparison of Haw Bridge with the Mythe Bridge emphasizes the genius of Thomas Telford, for it was built by a lesser man, who spanned the Severn with three iron arches on the site of the old Haw Passage. This was an ancient passage across the river where the channel was extremely shallow in the days before navigation weirs, and even to-day all traffic is compelled, through the shallowness of the river, to take the Tirley arch of the bridge. It is hard to see what essential purpose this bridge served at the time of its construction, since to-day it carries the minimum of motor traffic, as the road is not a link between any two towns, and before it was built the local countryside got along well enough without it. Indeed, when the bridge was completed, one Tirley farmer showed his contempt for the bridge, and his resentment at paying tolls, by fording and swimming the river on his horse, within shadow of the bridge, until the end of his days.

One of the most charming byways of the Severn is the Coombe Hill canal, so conspicuous on the map with its thick line of blue, yet almost lost to the passer-by in its overgrowth of greenery. It was built during the short era when enthusiasm for water transport reached such proportions that Tewkesbury even contemplated the project of linking itself with Cheltenham by canal.

This canal runs in the direction of Cheltenham, across as level a three miles of ground as any to be found on Severnside. So low-lying is this land that the canal was able to be worked without any lock, and barges made their way up here to dump their loads of coal at the foot of Coombe Hill, within four and a half miles of Cheltenham. Water from the Chelt was diverted to feed the canal and give enough draught for barges. In the winter months the canal fills up with water, and so low-lying are the surrounding meadows that they are the first to be flooded and the last to retain their flood-water of any lands on Severn.

45

The deserted canal is a natural haven for water plants, which prefer a more tranquil existence than the boisterous and turbulent life of the Severn. The bulrush, or more properly the reed-mace, makes a great and glorious showing here, and lovelier still, but far more shyly, blooms the flowering rush like a pink agapanthus lily, a plant worthy of any garden. These blooms come to take the place of the midsummer glories of the wild rose, which riots here unpruned and unadmired, and the yellow flag. On either side of this deserted waterway there is a free passage for the walker, who if he is not charmed by a kingfisher will almost certainly surprise a heron.

The canal is a haunt of the fox and the stoat. Indeed, one morning I met a stoat who was almost tame, for he ran to within five yards of me and then stood up on his hind legs. A strong wind was blowing from him to me, and as I stood quite still I was the mere image of a man of whom he had no fear. I sometimes think that animals judge their distance from another creature by their sense of smell and rely less on their sense of focus, as is the case with human beings. My presence was a bar to his progress. His whole body expressed something a human being expresses in its face, thoughtful curiosity, and I felt almost flattered when his fore-paws dropped to the ground and he skipped away through the grass with the leisurely grace of a cat.

The Chelt flows through Squire Hawkins's country to find the Severn between the canal and Wainlode Hill. No doubt the squire as he grew older drank for his body's health of the spring at Wainlode, for this spring is similar to the purging saline waters which made Cheltenham famous.

Wainlode presents as great a natural contrast in landscape as is to be seen anywhere, for the ground rises from the water's edge in a red, vertical cliff, streaked with grey, a hundred feet high. The finest aspect of this cliff is to be seen when coming down the river, for at this point the cliff is the cause of the river taking a sharp bend. It has a northern aspect and is usually to be seen in the sunless frown of its own shadow, which is almost beautiful as it throws into bolder relief the greenery of the fields and the red-brick comeliness of the nearby inn. The Romans came here and the road they made leading down to the river is still in use, for Wainlode is a favourite spot with Gloucester folk on summer afternoons.

The bare broad brow of Wainlode Hill is topped by woodland, through which the rambler must wander unless he is to take a wider detour, for the way be-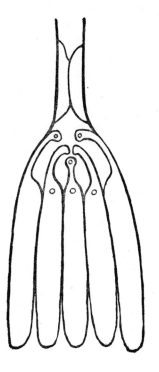tween the cliff and the river is slow and difficult. At one time a notice on the edge of this wood warned trespassers to beware of adders. I doubt if this was any proof of the viper's habitat; it was most probably placed there to discourage Eve when walking out with Adam.

But the peril of Wainlode is not in its adders but in the river, for many over - confident and inexperienced swimmers have been drowned here. Below the hill the river bed sinks into a great pit, so deep that the bargemen were unable to touch its bottom with the ends of their twenty-foot Severn shafts. This is the greatest depth in all the river, yet in the winter months it fills up with a sump of mud, and here many eels, who are not old enough to migrate to the sea, fatten and prosper. This knowledge was put to good account by some of the old fishermen who came here in winter, and many an eel saw the last of the river on the end of an eel-spear. This great weapon is still in use below Gloucester, and is like the flat, iron hand of a giant, whose fingers almost touch. This 'hand,' about nine inches wide and a foot long, is fastened to the end of a twenty-foot pole by which it is plunged into the mud, and on withdrawal, as often as not, an eel will be found caught between the fingers.

The only man I know above Gloucester to use an eel-spear is Arthur Payne of Tewkesbury, who had one made for him by his nephew, a toolmaker by trade. But this spear, unlike those of ancient pattern with their fingers almost touching, was shaped like a barbed five-pronged 'trident,' and Arthur after many attempts has failed to catch a single eel. Which shows that it needs more than enthusiasm to recapture an ancient craft once it has been lost.

In the slow-moving days of horse-drawn barges, urged on their way by Severn shafts, Wainlode Hill was a landmark to these inland mariners. A little up-river from the hill the river bank has become a fitting cemetery for a number of these old craft, which have been sunk here and filled with gravel and cement to prevent the encroachment of the river. The few Severn shafts still remaining, with a short iron prong on their river end, are kept to knock down the last apples at the top of the tree in cottage orchards. The passing of these craft has done to the river what the passing of the stage-coach did to the highways of England a century ago. For every public-house still on the river bank another has vanished for want of custom, since many of them relied entirely on passing trade. Here bargemen tied up for the night, drank their fill, and slept snug till dawn. Some of these were simple cider houses selling pure harsh apple juice, and became just cottages when barges hurried by towed by tugs and the nearest neighbour lived a mile away. Others, like the 'Fox and Goose' and the 'Jolly Waterman,' were, in the language of Langland, 'nales' selling beer.

As they worked the bed of the river with their Severn shafts, the bargees had an extraordinary knowledge of the river bed which has since been lost, and it is significant that they had a different name for almost every hundred yards of the river. These names were mostly unknown to all but those who used the river, and never having been written on a map have passed into oblivion.

Between Wainlode and Gloucester is one of the loneliest reaches of the river with hardly a cottage along the bank

EEL-NETS IN OCTOBER

until one is within sight of the city. Opposite Ashleworth church the footpath leading down to the ferry runs through a patch of jungle. Before the horse-ferry fell into decay this was a hard stone road and is worth looking at, for it shows the power of nature upon the work of man over a few short years. It should be seen by delegations of discouraged road-men, whose lives are spent sweeping up the leaves of autumn, the fallen blossoms of spring, the dusts of summer, and at all seasons the refuse of human negligence and animal necessity. They might look on this road and say, 'Without us the world would return to jungle and people to savages, from whom, with our view of human nature, we know them to be little removed.'

The road leads to the village of Sandhurst. Mushrooms abound on these pastures, but many cottagers in the village prefer 'blue-legs,' a fungus which comes into its own when the mushroom is on the wane, for it makes its first appearance with the first sharp frosts of October and continues in season up till Christmas. This fungus is dun-coloured on top, pale cream underneath, and its white stem is beautifully tinged with a delicate shade of heliotrope. To the nose it has the smell of ripe apricots, but after it has been cooked in the frying-pan and is served on the table it has the delicate flavour of the tenderest undercut of beef. This appetizing food wastes un-gathered in England's fields and meadows. The villagers round Sandhurst seldom touch blue-legs and they are not favoured in Gloucester; for this reason they would go to waste were it not for the number of retired tramps living at the lower end of Westgate Street, who go out and gather them and thereby pay their rent for many weeks to come. Blue-legs are sold locally and transported north, where they are appreciated on the tables of Yorkshire and Lancashire, and this trade is extensive enough for one old man to be known locally by the sobriquet of 'Blue-legs.'

The preference of the Sandhurst villagers for blue-legs, in defiance of surrounding prejudice, may perhaps originate from the abbots of Gloucester, who lived among them for four hundred years, since Ablode Court in this parish was the abbot's country house. The first abbot to come here was a Norman, who with a Frenchman's appreciative palate did not allow the blue-legs to go ungathered in his fields. He received this property along with other lands from King Henry I in exchange for an orchard under the abbey walls, whose trees grew where the present fifteenth-century perpendicular tower now stands. They must have been choice apples, or were possibly exceptionally good keepers, for which even in those days, according to William of Malmesbury, the Severn lands were famous; and Henry no doubt coveted them as Ahab coveted Naboth's vineyard.

Among Sandhurst characters is one old man who, because he is completely illiterate, is anxious on all occasions to conceal his ignorance. When he goes out into society, which for him is the public bar of the nearest inn, he never fails to pick up and peruse the Gloucester *Citizen*, and there is an even chance that you will catch him holding the paper upside down with an air of studious appraisal. His illiteracy has given him a strange caution; one morning over pints of cider I heard another old man ask him:

'How big would you say the mune is, Charlie?'

'Couldn't rightly say, Tom.'

'Would you say it was more nor less than a mile across?'

'Ah, I ain't saying, mid be more, mid be less.'

'Well, I 'm telling you it 's seventeen hundred miles across and they found that out nine thousand years ago.'

'Ah, there weren't many of us about nine thousand years ago,' said Charlie, nonchalantly turning his attention to the newspaper, dismissing the insinuation that he was nine thousand years behind the times.

VI. MINSTERWORTH

The Severn with a knife has pared the earth
Like Gloucester cheese from appled Minsterworth.

The fringe of Gloucester lies on an arm of the Severn at a point where the river becomes strangely devitalized by the city. Indeed, were it not for Maisemore River the Severn would lose most of its salmon, for few are the unwary fish who make the passage up the Gloucester river and survive, and many a silver fish floats on the surface of the receding tide, poisoned by Gloucester's drains.

The two streams join below Alney, and here the Severn gains fresh splendour, for the river is wider and the red banks higher. It is strange that this should be the greatest river in one of the most thickly populated countries of the world. No cottage or farmhouse stands on these fertile pastures, no fisherman sits with rod and line upon the river banks, and no craft of any kind is to be seen upon the water. This river is so dangerous and unpredictable that Gloucester's claim to call herself a port became nominal towards the end of the eighteenth century, until a Portuguese sea captain, worthy of the race that produced Vasco da Gama, sailed up the Severn to Gloucester with a cargo of port in 1791. The church bells of the city were rung in honour of this hero and his crew. As though inspired by this exploit, a ship canal between Gloucester and Sharpness was opened in 1827, reducing by half the long river voyage and eliminating countless dangers of navigation.

Similarly the road from Gloucester to Minsterworth more than halves the distance taken by the river, and for this reason few wander this way along its banks, yet this is one of the strangest and most fascinating walks in all England. On entering the meadows of Minsterworth parish, the wanderer turns to look at Gloucester and sees little or nothing of the city except the cathedral with its splendid tower, as it stands

51

out from among the trees of the foreground against the blue
background of the Cotswold hills. The tower is the earliest
example, and among the finest, of English Perpendicular
architecture, for this style originated inside the structure of
Gloucester's Norman abbey. It asserted itself in the magnificent fan tracery of the cloisters and reached its final
perfection in the tower, built in the middle of the fifteenth
century. Like every great work of art this tower is built of
superb material, hewn from the hills of its background. This
stone possesses an extraordinary lucent quality of absorbing
light, which is seen in its finest effects during a day of sunshine
and cloud. While the sun fills the landscape the tower looks
grey, but when the storm clouds hang over the hills it not only
appears white, but becomes the brightest thing in the whole
landscape, brighter even than the sky.

Leland, who saw the tower when it was less than a century
old, describes it as standing as 'a pharos to all parts around
for a considerable distance.' Indeed, the tower enhances one
of the greatest optical illusions I know, for after you have
apparently been walking away from it for an hour, the
cathedral confronts you again with disconcerting nearness.
And what is more, while the Cotswolds have been on your
left hand and May Hill on your right, their positions are now
reversed, and instead of looking towards the cathedral across
the river, green fields fill the foreground with the river on
your left. Furthermore, if the tide happens to be in flood, as
it is here on so many days of the year, the river seems to be
flowing backwards and you feel that you are indeed bewitched.
This amazing effect is caused through the river making a horseshoe bend, which being over several miles is so gradual as to
be unnoticed to the eye until startled by reality.

On the outer curve of this horseshoe bend of the river
stands the hamlet of Stonebench, which is the most popular
place for sightseers to view the Bore, for this is one of the few
places with a road frontage on Severn tide. Visitors sometimes get more than they bargain for with wet feet. Time
and tide wait for no man, and the Bore, irrespective of

licensing hours, would burst into the bar of the Stonebench inn and may do so still, though this house has become a private dwelling.

Stonebench is a hamlet of Elmore and takes its name not from any seat from which the traveller can await the Bore at his ease, but from the ledge of rock running across the bed of the river. This submerged rock has the effect of combing the mane of the Bore into a finer crest, and at one time the Stonebench was used as a ford, though a dangerous one.

I sometimes wonder how the sight of the Bore affects different people. There is a tradition on Severn side, and I have no doubt that it is based upon fact, for the original Silurian stock to the west of the river has survived the centuries, that the Romans when first they saw the Bore thought that the end of the world was at hand. No one is ever likely again to experience this sensation, but to all who are truly alive a good Bore comes bringing with it a faint sense of atavistic panic and leaves behind it a feeling of magic and wonder. Experience and tide-tables can never wholly rid my mind of the thought that somehow this wonder of nature will one day exceed itself, so that every time the Bore passes me I am left with a sense of disappointment and relief that it has not swept me off my feet from where I stand on Severn's bank.

There are still a few who greet the Bore with physical defiance. One of them is Webb, the fisherman of Madam Pool; long familiarity with the Bore through the best part of half a century has given his face the unsmiling expression of a beardless Neptune. He now rides the wave in his punt, but in his younger days it was his pleasure and his pride to swim the Bore as it swept past his acres. I do not think that this heroic gesture is as hazardous as it looks to those who know the river. Though I have never seen it done, I warn any of my readers who are strong swimmers against following his example. Any attempt to meet the Bore other than head-on might prove fatal, for the wave would probably keep a man under long enough to drown him.

Webb the fisherman is a farmer, but he fishes Madam Pool

with a long-net and this is about the best long-net fishery on the Severn. It is never disturbed by passing river traffic; the river is at this point exceptionally narrow and the drag is not more than two hundred yards long. High tides, which here can be very appreciable, often prevent fishing for several days; the tide itself does not interfere with fishing, but the fish do not travel on the stronger tides.

Madam Pool long-net differs from those used above Gloucester, for no swill or cod is knit into it, and judging by results I doubt if many fish are lost by these omissions. When the salmon hits the net, it is against his nature to turn and swim downstream, nor in such a position has he the opportunity to leap the net. It is a common sight in early summer to see salmon leaping for a split second in the quiet water below the pool, but it is very rare to see one leap when once imprisoned by the horseshoe formed by the net, because by then he is almost certainly held by the fold of the net caused by this contraction.

There is nothing to distinguish the working owner of a fishery from his men. He has no need to give orders, for each man knows his job, and with each successive drag a change is made in the stations to relieve the monotony and to equalize the labour. The muntle man, however, remains at his post throughout on the opposite bank to save the trouble of constant ferrying. This has always seemed to me the most strenuous job of all. One day, watching an old man pulling the muntle during a hot summer's afternoon without relief, I remarked on this and was told: 'We keep him there because he's old and there's not so much for him to do.' Certainly he had long rests while the net was being pulled in and relaid, but all the same it looks like hard work to me.

'Here comes Fishy,' says one of the men, with contempt in his voice. A figure from the city is seen crossing the meadow. He is no honest fishmonger, but is either a local glutton or black-marketeer. On his arrival he is received in silence by the fishermen, who neither look at him nor pause in the rhythm of their work. He struts up and down the bank in his

LONG-NET FISHING AT MADAM POOL

shirt sleeves, posing as though he owned the fishery. Irritated
by his idle attitude and patronizing pose, the fisherman who
heralded his approach reminds him in the curtest tone that
he is only 'a bloody publican.' If Fishy had had the good
sense or the good fellowship to arrive with a few bottles of
beer, the taunt would have lost its point, but he has neither
the spirit to answer back nor the dignity to go his way.

As the net is being drawn in he stands a few feet from the
flake, with greed in his eye and anxiety upon his face; his pose
is now that of an active supporter and patron of a manly
sport. The net is finally drawn in on to the flake, in it there
are three fair-sized fish, they are quickly killed, but none of
them are for Fishy.

He goes away defeated, disappointed, and unashamed, and
in an hour's time behind a beer-engine he will be telling men
as stupid as himself of the day's sport he had salmon fishing.

The grassy bank of the sea wall between Gloucester and
Minsterworth is no guarantee against freshwater floods, and
when the river is full the Bore will top this five-foot rampart
of turf surmounting the red marl of the river bank. At such
times it is an impressive sight to watch the green meadows
turning to silver in a matter of moments. Minsterworth
church is the last place along Severn tide to be affected by
'freshes,' as freshwater floods are called on the lower river,
and this fact is heralded by Minsterworth's many orchards.
In the Severn landscape, full of heavy timber, a pear orchard
in full blossom hides and hints at the presence of a farmhouse. In spring it reflects the passing glory of an April day,
as under the sun it gleams with terrestrial light, dazzling the
sky. Then with the passing of a cloud the light vanishes from
the blossom as it hangs grey and heavy with the promise of
its own maturity under the shadow of the sky.

Minsterworth is one of the comparatively few villages named
on Speed's earliest map of Gloucestershire, perhaps for the
simple and naïve reason that the parish is long and narrow,
and permitted the pen of the cartographer to letter the name
within the parish boundaries. There is, however, an indication

that the village was as thickly populated then as it is now. Samuel Rudder writes of a custom, ancient and obsolete in his day, and peculiar to this village, whereby every householder paid a toll of twopence a year to the lord of the manor. This rate, known as smoke silver, was paid by as many as a hundred houses in Minsterworth.

To-day the village glows with the easy prosperity of small holdings, for the Severn in the past has raised many a cottager to the independent status of a small yeoman.

A familiar link between Severnside villages is the periwinkle scrambling through cottage hedgerows. This lovely flower blooms shyly, but with the virtue of flowering at most times of the year. As a child I disliked the periwinkle, despising its queer choice of blooming in unfavoured places; since then I have gradually learnt to love the plant with its smooth, green leaf and the bloom of its eye, which is unmatched in the tones of sky or sea, or in any other flower of the field or garden. It is the perfect flower of the cottage hedgerow; half wild, it holds the frontier between the garden and the farm.

Architecturally Minsterworth is without distinction, and it is the river and orchards that give the village its character. Minsterworth is a curiously independent village with a taste for trade with foreign parts. A sixty-year-old man repairing the river bank told me how puzzled he had been as a child at hearing his grandmother ask a passing bargee to bring her back a 'nest of pans' from Bridgwater, since these utensils were made in the Somersetshire town and could be bought more cheaply there than in Gloucester. The village rarely sold its fruit in Gloucester market where prices were low, but exported it to Newport in Sam Wathan's sloop, and Minsterworth was mightily proud of the fact that its merchant navy was able to dock in Newport harbour free of dues, for the village being in the Duchy of Lancaster is absolved from paying dues and tolls in harbours and markets. No privilege appeals to countrymen more than one which allows them to go free where others have to pay, and being in the duchy has made

Minsterworth a village of haughty, mellow folk. This parish became part of the duchy through John of Gaunt's marriage with Blanche of Lancaster, whose early death at the age of twenty-nine inspired Chaucer to write *The Book of the Duchesse*. Elmore Back, across the water from Minsterworth, is also part of the duchy, for until recently it was part of the same parish, but there being no ferry between these parts of the village Elmore Back was transferred to the parish whose name it bears.

Yet men have walked across the river between Elmore Back and Minsterworth, for they are linked by a submerged shelf known as Church Rock, broken in the centre by a gully so narrow that it may be straddled by a man. In dry summers this rock has been seen above water, and here on dark nights many a salmon has been poached by the Welsh method of gaffing, which demands such quickness and skill that a man who takes a salmon by this means deserves it. A gaffing-iron, which is fastened to a stick, is a C-shaped hook with a sharp barb on its end. The poacher walked out along Church Rock, bestrode the gully like the Colossus of Rhodes, and in this position smote the ascending salmon on its side with his gaffing-iron as it shot between his legs.

Poachers of this calibre are born, not made, and it is a good many years since Church Rock has shown above water to make this exploit possible. Still in most summers the ascending salmon may at times be seen jumping out of the water for no apparent reason as they leap over Church Rock. A good deal of mud accumulates above the rock, and eel-spears are still used in Minsterworth where they are to be seen lying idle on either side of the river throughout the summer months. They stand with their iron fingers touching the ground as their twenty-foot shafts lean among the orchard trees.

About a mile below Church Rock the Dinny Rock runs under the Severn, and so much sand collected against it that old folk in Minsterworth still remember the time when this was their playground and they were almost able to walk across the Severn. Now this rock is never seen, though an

c

unevenness in the water sometimes gives a hint of its existence. In the late 1930s a large school of dolphins entered the Severn never to return. As many as forty-seven, a conservative estimate, were counted entering Minsterworth water. They lingered here for a number of days, unable to return to the sea through being imprisoned by the barrier of these rocks, until they finally died either through want of salt water or lack of their proper food.

The cottage known as the 'Shark' at Elmore Back, a little above the Dinny, most probably commemorates the un-recorded taking of a shark by a long-net in these waters, since sharks have from time to time been taken in the lower Severn. The 'Shark,' half hidden among orchards, was a cider house which, until it went out of business sixty years ago, lived up to its name. It was a rendezvous of smugglers, ideally situated on the river, away from any road. Bargees came here to quench their thirst and leave behind kegs of liquor finer than anything they drank at the 'Shark.' The bargees picked up their contraband of French brandy or Dutch hollands from merchantmen in the Bristol Channel, and the 'Shark' had an unquenchable thirst for unbroached casks, which looked as innocent as pickpockets where cider barrels can stand as thick as skittles in an alley without arousing comment.

A local band of men found regular employment in carrying contraband from the 'Shark' to London, and when one considers the enormous popularity of Severn cider in the London of former days, their journeys can have aroused small suspicion. Their activities were, however, so well known locally that their homes, for they were all neighbours, were given the nickname of 'Rogues' Row.'

VII. FRAMILODE

The river as it leaves Minsterworth flows through some of its loveliest reaches as it enters Westbury parish and passes the extensive hamlets of Bollo and Rodley.

Both banks are gay with colourful birds. They are the birds classified as common by the ornithologist, but ones that can never be common to the eye of the beholder, greenfinches, bullfinches, goldfinches, and blue-tits as multitudinous as sparrows in a city street. They are to be seen at their best in the early days of spring, when their plumage is brightest and uneclipsed by leaves, while the remaining leaves of the bramble spray by contrast enhance the colour of the pairing blue-tits. The pear-trees cause the tits to congregate here in even greater numbers in the autumn, when the teasel is the special lure of the goldfinch. The teasel is a common weed the length of Severn tide, for at one time the plant was culti-vated at Westbury for the benefit of the cloth mills at Stroud.

But surpassing these little birds in size and splendour is the green woodpecker, who in his relative solitude is the emperor of them all. The woodpecker mates for life, and possibly on this account he quickly grows tired of female companion-ship, for how rarely one sees him other than alone. You will hardly walk through any Severnside orchard without dis-turbing the apple-green yaffle, who fills his domain with his laughter from the New Year until apples are ripe. Sometimes his body gleams golden in the sun, and by his resemblance to the parrot he gives an almost tropical atmosphere to his surroundings. But the intimate bird-life of Bollo changes with the altering landscape as the river widens into the broad expanse of Longney sands. Here the river bank is being eaten away as the sands in the river-bed increase. As often as not you will see five or six cormorants, squatting like black cats on the edge of the water, or drifting with the current across the shallows. Crows and plovers strut upon these acres as though to prophesy by their walk that one day these sand-banks will be green islands.

As you look north from here you catch an unexpected view of the blue rump of the Malvern Hills, with which the land across the river has a territorial link, for the manor of Longney once belonged to the priory of Great Malvern. Longney, once famed for its 'fine cheese and stout cider,' has given its name to the Longney russet, an apple which is an exceptionally good keeper that will remain sound 'till apples come again.' Longney is still faithful to this apple, which has lost much of its ancient popularity and fame, for to-day you will find few Longney russets outside this parish. Framilode takes its beautiful name from the lode or emptying of the river Frome into the Severn. This is the last lode downstream, for below here, owing to the daily flushing of the tide, these creeks are known as pills. But for several days in the month, around the neap tide, there is no tide at Framilode, for it takes eighteen feet of water at Sharpness to show an inch of tide at Framilode.

The unnavigable Frome gave power to the cloth mills at Stroud and made the scarlet dye of that town famous, until Stroud in the interest of her trade cut a canal forty-two feet wide to Framilode. This waterway, eight miles long, completed after four years' labour in 1779, opened up the ambitious project of linking the Thames and Severn by canal. Twenty years later the canal was continued to the Thames at Inglesham, a mile above Lechlade, passing on its way through a tunnel a mile and a half long, which pierced he Cotswolds at Sapperton. The canal turned Framilode from a hamlet into a village, as a floating population of recurringly familiar faces waited either in the river or in the canal for the coming of the tide. Framilode became the home of many a bargee. The canal prospered for forty years until the competition of the railways began. In 1841 it carried nearly ninety thousand tons and took £11,330 in receipts, in return for an investment which had cost less than £250,000. In the days of its decline the canal was bought by the railway,

who kept it in a state of quiescence until it was bought for
£19,000 by a public trust for whom it earned £271. Now
the canal is dry, except for the original Stroudwater canal,
which is linked to the river through the Gloucester–Berkeley
canal, for since 1920 the canal's entrance to the Severn at
Framilode has been sealed by a wall of concrete. This
provides Framilode with a pleasant backwater, which gives
the village a Venetian air; not the Venice of the tourist
but the rural Venetia of the lagoons, a fantasy heightened by
the Italianate architecture of the Victorian parish church.
The little village, unvexed by passing traffic, gives rare
pleasure to the eye as it stands, alone of villages of the vale,
on the very brink of the Severn. The winding lode with its
banks of slippery mud would be a detraction to the village
were it not for the bright kingfisher, who glows like a jewel
among the osiers or boldly faces you with his breast of red,
so that you are hardly aware of his presence among the shades
of dun and brown that surround him. He leaves the pill to
take his evening flight under the east bank of the river a
couple of hours before sunset, pausing for a moment to dive
upon a basking shrimp. He is a rarity along this stretch of
river and shows by his presence Framilode's comparative
immunity from flood. The channel, broadening as it does
here below Longney Point, is capable of carrying many times
the volume of water that hurries past Minsterworth, and only
exceptional sea tides top the river bank. Occasionally, however, Framilode receives the double attack of the river forces
in full fury when a 'fresh,' or land flood, descends upon a
rising spring tide and Framilode is outwitted by the Severn.
In one cottage on such an occasion the kettle was floated off
the hob. The village stands unprotected by sea wall, and
only a miniature village green, no larger than a garden lawn,
divides it from the river. The only protection offered against
erosion is that given by the old sunk boat such as salmon
fishermen use downstream, appropriately known as a stopping
boat, filled with stones and grounded against the garden of
the cottage nearest the river.

The Severn has less power against Framilode than against any level ground between Gloucester and the sea. The sea tide is much weakened when it reaches Framilode, but gains new strength a mile higher up when it enters a narrower channel. Natural prejudice against the river bank prevented any village being built at Framilode until the cutting of the canal, and the church dates from after the beginning of the canal's decline. But Framilode had some little importance in the Middle Ages, when its fishery, belonging to the abbey of Gloucester, was leased to the abbot of Winchcombe for £4 a year, a handsome consideration in those days. To-day no one makes a living by fishing at Framilode, though they were using the long-net here as recently as 1937. The river still provides the village with a variety of food and individuals with handsome windfalls. Elvers are not as plentiful as they were, but their value has increased out of all proportion to their decrease in quantity, and Framilode men, who in the past have hawked this fry at 1½d. a pound through the villages, have lived to see their catches collected from them for the Cardiff market and have received 2s. 3d. a pound. Before the war Framilode sold its surplus of elvers to a German at Epney, who exported them alive to stock the German rivers. This business was started before the First World War and was resumed after the peace until 1939; now it is controlled by the Ministry of Agriculture and Fisheries, who in one year took half a million elvers from the Severn and dumped them into the upper Thames between Lechlade and Oxford.

At one time the Thames was a salmon and eel river, but not even eels can pass the barrage of London sewers. Elvers, however, continued to reach the Thames from Framilode to Inglesham through the canal. But though the eel is able to travel a considerable distance overland the present condition of the canal has long made this journey impossible.

Framilode would seem half asleep were it not for the watchful eye of old George. Leisure and a good pair of binoculars give an air of opulence to his workaday appearance,

ELVERING

and the cast-off G.P.O. linesman's overalls he wears lend
comparative youthfulness to his eighty years. The small
gold rings in his ears hint of the romance of distant places.
The droop of his moustache betokens the inward arrogance
of a man who has been accustomed to command. His deep,
low voice has an almost Shakespearian familiarity with the
English language, for he has a genius for adorning his conversation with the exact and unexpected adjective.

He sits all day long on top of Framilode's river bank, a
solitary figure in the sun, or else like some phantom ship's
figure-head looming out of the autumn mists when seen
across the river. He surveys the moving water and no motion
of fish or fowl escapes his eye, for the river runs as a continuous
thread through his long life. He has been bargemaster,
fisherman, and waterfowler. As a youth of nineteen he often
sailed past Framilode as skipper of a barge. Then as soon as
'things began to go wrong' he would go to sea, always to
return in two or three years' time as a salmon to the Severn.
Some of the best years of George's life have been spent as a
salmon fisherman. In the summer of 1912 he averaged thirty
salmon a day, in the month of July, when fish sold at tenpence a
pound. In those days a fisherman might make as much money
in a week as a farm labourer would in a year.

Though Framilode is one of the ancient passages or ferries
across the Severn, George when he retired from the sea started
another ferry and founded a reputation for ferrying any one
any hour in any weather. Once at three in the morning he
was roused by two young couples returning from a dance.
It was a night 'thick as a bag.' It was only by familiarity
that George was able to fumble for his boat, and then he had to
return to the cottage for his compass, relic of his seafaring days.
With the aid of the compass he grounded the Rodley shore and
even then the revellers could not find their way up the bank.
So George took his compass and steered for the top of the bank,
dragging an oar behind him through the mud to guide his
passengers and to leave a trail for his return. His passengers
paid him 'half a quid,' the highest fare he has ever received.

George is the only man I know in Framilode who rides the
Bore, an operation which is sometimes necessary when it is
impossible to pull a heavy boat out of the tideway. To do
this he rows downstream for a mile to meet the Bore and
with his back to the wave pulls into the Bore, which lifts the
boat so that it rides like a porpoise into the tide. If he was
to meet the Bore at Framilode he would be carried far upstream and have to wait for the turn of the tide to carry him
home. Many fatal accidents have been caused through failing
to meet the Bore head on, and even experienced rivermen
have lost their lives when in their over-confidence they have
taken the wave at an angle and been overturned.

At Framilode the Bore may be watched for seven or eight
minutes, but it takes an experienced eye to recognize a three-
or even a four-foot wave at a distance of two miles, for the
Bore between Newnham and Arlingham flows as smoothly as
curving glass, and only where it dashes against the sides of
the river bed does it attract attention.

Between Arlingham and Garden Cliff the river bed is half
a mile wide, but less than a quarter of a mile at Upper Framilode, where there is a drop of about ten to twelve feet from
the grass verge to the surface of the river at low water. Amid
this waste of mud and sand the river winds like a snake, sliding
under Garden Cliff and then cutting across the ascending
rapids to Arlingham, where the channel is known as Unla
Water.

Upon so vast a stage it is not easy for the Bore to make a
big showing, and the flood-head of the wave hardly seems to
wet the sand as it splashes either side of the main channel.
But this is a great deception, for the eye is naturally engrossed
by the oncoming wave, yet when it looks back a second or
two later it sees that the sand-banks are covered and that the
bed of the river is an unbroken sheet of water.

The Bore arrives mildly enough at Framilode, dwarfed as
it is by the river bank, yet awe-inspiring when one sees with
what force it dashes against the stopping boat, protecting the
river bank at the cottage garden. It is then that great things

begin in the river. With the speed and grace of skaters skimming the ice, a smooth sheet of water covers the broad sand flat across the river. This is utterly unlike the commonplace incoming of the tide on the seashore, for with this wave there is no immediate ebb. Where there was a firm bed of sand there is in less than two minutes a great whirlpool, fifty yards wide, caused through the tide over the sand meeting the channel tide. The whirlpool mounts higher and higher against the opposite bank as the river rises, as though two people were in argument and refusing to move with the crowd. The movement of this whirlpool reminds me of a young dog running great circles in a meadow of grass, for the whirlpool turns at about the same speed and describes a similar circle. Elsewhere the Bore has caused other disturbances. Half a mile away a ground race has been caused by the tide breaking over the sands of Priding's Point, where the surface of the river is broken by clusters of waves five feet high. These ground-race waves are entirely local and die on the bed of their birth; for all their showing they add not a ripple to the hurrying flow past Framilode and are overlain by the tide that bore them.

After about ten minutes the Framilode whirlpool, overcome by the weight of opinion behind it, joins the flowing tide. But the surface of the water off Framilode is still troubled, over two or three acres of river the water is broken by scores of dancing waves. They are the waves which people imagine, but never see, when thinking of a choppy sea, for they are short broken water, jumping two or three feet high, yet making no progress. These waves are called the fiddles, for they make the river dance. They are pointed as the thorns on a rose-bush and their appearance is remarkable, for the pattern of their motion is entirely surrounded by smooth unbroken water. After about a quarter of an hour the fiddles are followed by the rudder, long low waves undulating diagonally across the river. The rudder tide, so called because its motion resembles the passing of a phantom ship, only lasts for a few minutes and with its passing the

* C

flow of the tide continues undisturbed. By now the river is nearing fullness. A few yards from the opposite bank a full-grown salmon leaps from the water like a silver sixpence tossed by an unseen hand from underneath the water — the only sign of animal or bird life the Bore has shown with its passing.

In less than an hour a channel twelve feet deep and a quarter of a mile wide has filled with water, so that the beholder can bend down from the river bank and wash his hands—then an incredible thing happens, the level of the water begins to drop while the tide continues to flow upstream. The flow continues for ten minutes, yet the river has dropped six inches from high water. In the last quarter of an hour the tide has lost appreciable speed until it finally ceases, so that a piece of wood that has been carried upstream floats motionless in the middle of the river as though it lay on the surface of a horse-pond. There is a dead calm on the river for five minutes, then gradually the piece of wood moves downstream; in another five minutes the tide is in swift ebb. Yet at this moment the Bore is still running, and is now passing Gloucester and will run for another forty minutes, shrunk like a salmon after spawning to the ghost of what it was, until it dashes fretfully against the wooden gates of Tewkesbury Lock.

At Framilode the tide comes in an hour and ebbs for eleven hours, and with the turn of the tide you may hear the hooting of ships and barges at Frampton-on-Severn, which entered the Gloucester–Berkeley canal when it was high water at Sharpness and now warn the bridge-keeper of their approach.

Before the opening of the canal all up-river traffic on the Severn was dependent on the Bore, or at least on a good tide. There are few men left to-day with knowledge to navigate the river between Sharpness and Gloucester. Old George claims to be the last of the river pilots and with him will die more knowledge of the river than is ever likely to be learnt again. It is especially dangerous to travel on a Bore tide, because even when the surface of the water looks safe only a man with complete knowledge of the river-bed may navigate without courting disaster. As soon as a boat travelling on the Bore grounds or even grazes a sand-bast, the Bore lifts the boat from the water and rolls it over and over.

If an ordinary dinghy or stopping-boat was launched just after the flood head of the Bore had passed and was steered without oars on the tide, it would travel upstream for about eight miles. It would be carried up in passive resistance against the force of the tide but, owing to the suction of the boat's belly against the water, it would not keep pace with the Bore and would drop back into slackening water until it came to a final standstill.

The old experienced Severn barge- and trow-men made the voyage from Sharpness to Gloucester, some twenty-six miles, in about two hours, which compares favourably with the time taken by motor-barges over little more than half that distance in the canal. When one considers that these bargemen used oars and pulled incredible weights, even discounting the exceptional forces of nature ruling in the Severn, their exploits have a Homeric quality, which pales the Oxford and Cambridge boat race to the academics of watermanship. Barges and trows heavily laden, usually with Chepstow stone, were towed by a tow-boat. This had to be filled with half a ton of stone as ballast to keep it well down in the water and to prevent it from being jerked back to the barge in tow.

The Bore was given a start to give the river a body of water for the voyage. The tow-boat was pulled and navigated by eighteen-foot-long oars of oak. By this means the waterman kept pace with the flood-head of the Bore, running a mile or so ahead of them, while the barge for all its weight ran behind them like a torpedo, for it was narrow and long, offering the minimum of suction to the river.

The coasts of Rodley, Longney, Bollo, Minsterworth, and Elmore are thick with orchards, each as large as a good-sized field, and a good idea of the pace of these voyages may be gained from the saying of the old watermen, which George repeated to me as I stood beside him while we watched the passing Bore: 'We used to say we took an orchard at a stroke when pulling a barge.' Words that will nevermore be repeated on Severnside.

'If the young fellows of to-day,' he went on, with the eternal prerogative of old age, 'had to do what we had to do, they'd be dead, yes, they'd be dead. Being brought up rough, that's what makes you last. When I was a boy I went to sea so young that when I filled the ship's kettle I wasn't man enough to lift it on the fire. Many's the time I've been out all night on the river in a little boat and never troubled to come home. I haven't slept in a bed for forty years. I turn up rough, just as I am, like a trooper's horse on the sofa.'

Sometimes George remembers bores met in the darkness of a winter's night, and horror comes into his voice like the choke of distant thunder on a summer afternoon.

'I've been out on Frampton Sands wild-fowling of a night and a thick bank of fog has come down so as you can hardly see the end of the boat. And I've heard the tide roaring down by Sharpness, and an awful dread has come over me, and I've sat and waited in my boat and the wait has seemed like hours, though perhaps it was only twenty minutes.'

Unless you know George and Frampton Sands you could hardly understand how such circumstances should arise, or why a man should sit and wait in great fear for twenty minutes, which seemed like hours, without attempting to escape. Under normal circumstances the Bore had no terror for George and would on this occasion be used as part of the afternoon's campaign, which worked to a time table contrived by nature, for the Bore would carry him home. He would slip downstream from Framilode on the ebb tide to out below the Noose. He would then have travelled eight or nine miles, though only two or three as the wild duck flies across the Arlingham penisula. He would arrive at his hunting ground at three in the afternoon, the hour when the wild geese, which have been feeding on the meadows and open marsh lands of New Grounds, think of returning to the river. This is the marksman's hour; by four the light is not so good, by

five o'clock it has failed, though even then you may get a
lucky shot.

A blood-red sun, sinking out of a clear blue sky behind the
black lace of the oaks of the Forest of Dean's skyline, is no
promise of a clear night on the river, or that a wild-goose
moon, that should attend the rising Bore, will not be obscured
by fog. At such times the waterman will have to wait for
the Bore, like many a more prosaic sportsman for the train,
to carry him home, and for this he must wait until half-past
eight or nine in the evening, since to row home against the
rapids of Unla Water is impossible.

The dangers of meeting the Bore in the dark are twofold.
To overcome a foe you must ride forth to meet him, so with
the Bore a man must row into it and must ride like a man
riding to water on a horse, fast and straight. If he strikes it
at an angle he is doomed, and it is no easy matter to strike
straight at the unseen or to judge the instant of encounter.
The other great danger is to be caught by the Bore as it is
passing a mud-bast or sand-bank. These temporary islands
are of irregular shape, so that the Bore whips round one side
faster than the other, and if the boat happens to be caught
on the meeting of the waters it is lifted up and rolled over on
its back.

Instinct, which governs the lives of wild things on the
Severn, must have stood by George on these occasions when
skill and experience cast a shadow over natural confidence.
Lesser men might at such times have abandoned ship and
run for shore, but this would mean leaving the boat to become
a total wreck, nor even with twenty minutes to spare might
any man be certain in a river fog of finding the bank before
the tide caught him, where the river with pools and quicksands is a mile and a half wide. Here a man might wander
in panic terror while listening to the gentle roar of the
approaching wave.

They were moments of dread followed by exaltation for
George as he rode the Bore in the dark. Heroic moments,
unseen by any eye beneath the blanket of fog, as pulling hard

he rowed against the knife-edge of the tide to be borne triumphantly home upon its mounting shoulders. Home on such nights as these often meant the shelter and security of his boat, for it is easier to jump on to a platform from a train as it roars through a station, than to make a safe mooring when swept up-river by the Bore. The stillness of the tide might come when he reached Framilode, unrecognizable in the fog, or he might be carried past the village up to Longney, but with the ebb he would find haven on the sands till daybreak.

A man may shoot wildfowl from a boat provided the boat is afloat on the tideway, but if the boat is aground, or the fowler is standing in the water, he is poaching. This finding was threshed out in the Court of Chancery in 1908, when Fitzhardinge, lord of the manor of Berkeley, brought an action against Purcell, to restrain Purcell from shooting wild-fowl on the river in the manor of Berkeley. Consequently the wild-fowler stalks his game in a boat, and river cunning rather than sporting sentiment is the order of the day in the river.

One winter's afternoon George fired with both barrels on a flock of geese where they stood thickest on a mud-bast. He picked up a dozen geese and another two were picked up later a couple of miles away. At another time he brought down five with two shots, when confused in a fog at twilight they came down all of a cluster in the lime-trees between the river and Framilode church. A shot like that was made possible by keeping his gun hidden under the tarpaulin in his boat. Sometimes he shoots a cormorant, for this bird is the favourite dish of an old fellow in the neighbouring village of Saul, who scalds and skins his bird before cooking it.

The only fishing George does nowadays is to catch passing timber as it floats down-river. He scrutinizes each piece of drift-wood through his binoculars, and if it has a 'label' on it the chances are that he will let it go by. For, says George, when he sees a formidable tree-stump: 'There's one with a label on it and the label means work.' In the course of a year he collects several tons of this timber, more than enough for his needs, which he stacks round the apple-tree in his garden. Here among the half-rotten drift-wood is the rusty head of an eel-spear. It was given to George many years ago by an old fisherman as he lay dying, and the gift carried with it much that was left unspoken. The old fellow would no longer prod the mud of ditches and pills on winter afternoons to return home at dusk with a basketful of eels, and in giving George his eel-spear he was taking farewell of life and handing on a tradition.

Eel-spearing here is confined to the pills and ditches, as no eel lies about in the sands of the river shallows, and perhaps for this reason eel-spearing has never appealed to George. From time to time a curio merchant tries to buy this spear and is always refused, for Neptune would as soon think of parting with his trident as George with his trophy, belonging as it does to the traditional life of the river.

Old George sometimes makes me think of Charon, not because he is a ferryman or on account of the dog who accompanies him in the boat when crossing the river, but because at all times and at all seasons he keeps vigil on the Severn. Sometimes from the Rodley bank I have seen him through the November mists, seated on the river bank like a phantom in another world. I have called to him and he, because he is a trifle deaf, or because in the past he has rowed across for nothing in answer to the shouts of puppy-love of boys and girls on holiday, pays little heed, nor through the winter mist can he identify me with the binoculars which are in his hands. Finally he comes, and though he knows me well and we have sat and talked for many hours discussing the river, he will hardly say as much as good morning until we are half way across.

But when George tells me of the awful dread that has filled him when listening and waiting for the tide in the darkness and loneliness of starless winter nights, I know that I am talking to one who has crossed the Styx and that Charon and his passenger are one.

I once asked George what his strangest find had been in
the way of river flotsam, and was surprised when he told me
that he had found nothing more interesting or useful than a
plank of wood. Half an hour after leaving him I came across
the most interesting thing that the Severn had cast ashore for
many a day, for drinking my tea in a Framilode tea-garden
I saw a coracle covered in mud.

'Who made the coracle?' I asked.

'Is that what you call it,' said Mrs. Smith. 'That's a bit
of rubbish my son fished out of the river last Sunday.'

It was shaped like a walnut-shell, except that it had a flat
bottom, and was four feet nine inches long, three feet wide,
and fourteen inches deep. The coracle was constructed of
thin laths of ash wood, covered in unbleached calico, which
had received several coats of tar. A stout board, nine inches
wide, spanning it from gunwale to gunwale, provided a not
uncomfortable seat and gave extraordinary strength to this
egg-shell of a craft. A strong leather strap was attached to
this seat, enabling the boat to be carried across the shoulders.
The rim of the coracle had been broken and there was a
small tear in the bottom of the vessel.

I knew of no coracle on the tidal Severn and was amazed
that one should have arrived here in so good a state of
preservation, for I imagined that this coracle had been swept
out of one of the Carmarthenshire rivers and carried by sea
and tide to Framilode. I left Framilode with some reluctance,
and would have made an offer for the coracle had I not a
long walk and two bus rides ahead of me before reaching
home. But the coracle would not leave me. I thought of
restoring it or making one like it and using it on some of
the unnavigable waterways of England, for when the water
becomes unnavigable, even for a coracle, you can pick up
your boat and walk. Some days later I returned to Framilode
and bought the coracle. I was now faced with the problem
of getting it home to Cirencester. I had come by train to
Stonehouse with a bicycle. I succeeded in riding with the
coracle on my back as far as Frampton, where I providentially

got a puncture, otherwise I might have had an accident, since the coracle acted as a sail and more than once the cycle was out of control.

I carried my coracle on my back and pushed my cycle to Stonehouse station. I shall never forget the superior look of amused tolerance on the face of a prim, bespectacled clerk as he passed me by. It was the crass look of one whose only criterion of civilization is a crude comparison with the primitive. On my way I made friends with several interested boys, and in Stonehouse a small child shouted with excitement: 'Look, mummy, a ship.'

The coracle was the cradle of our island history, and this humble craft was no hybrid but had been made in the unbroken tradition of thousands of years. Only the materials had changed, for its ancestor was a buckskin stretched across a frame of withy.

The Gloucester Folk Museum, which stands only a few hundred yards from Westgate Bridge, has a fine collection of Severnside exhibits and several models of coracles still in use. I have learnt from these that my coracle is not a South Wales type, but a true Severn coracle, for this 'bowl'-shaped variety of coracle has persisted round Ironbridge until the present day. When the first modern bridge, which gave Ironbridge its name, was built it paradoxically renewed the lease of the coracle age, when villagers objected to paying a penny to cross the bridge. Consequently almost every cottager owned a coracle which hung on an apple-tree, within view of his door. Coracles have another use, that of catching rabbits in time of flood, and for this reason the coracle has continued in the midlands to this day.

There are two places in Framilode where at low tide a man can walk across the river. The higher crossing at Epney is known as Cobbe's Rock. This is a dangerous crossing as there is deep water beside the rock. The lower crossing is Priding's Point where you may cross without getting your knees wet. At Cobbe's Rock there is no landmark to navigate the traveller, but those who seek it may stumble upon it in the vicinity of the solitary white house on the river bank between Framilode and

Epney. At Priding's Point you may cross by keeping in absolute alignment with your eye the chimneys of the only cottages to be seen in Rodley. These crossings are only to be recommended to good swimmers with knowledge of the tides.

Priding, a small hamlet, received its quaint name from the pride or prid, for so the lamprey was called in the seventeenth century by no less an authority than Isaac Walton, and prid gavel was a custom whereby fishermen paid the lordship of Rodley dues for the privilege of fishing for lampreys. Gavel is an obsolete word for rent. The method of catching lampreys here and at Minsterworth was unique. The lamprey swims near the surface, and to catch him in a weel a crib was built out into the river from the bank. These cribs were rectangles of mud and brushwood six yards by four, built into a level plateau to within a few inches of the surface of the water. Upon each crib was set a row of weels.

These cribs are now no longer made, but I have talked to middle-aged men who have built them, and who have made £5 in a tide from the lamperns taken there. This ingenious method of catching a fish which is now seldom eaten was due to the royal appetites in the Middle Ages, when Gloucester was under an obligation to supply the king with lampreys on his accession and every year at Christmas. King John fined the men of Gloucester 40 marks, £12 13s. 4d., because they did not pay him sufficient respect in the matter of his lampreys. The basket was used to catch the fish in preference to the net to save the lampreys being bruised, for when caught they were often kept alive for long periods in baskets, known as hard weels, which were sunk in the river.

The lamprey, a scarce fish, was always an anxiety to someone in Gloucester for at least six centuries. Nor was it to be had for nothing. The lamprey pies supplied to the king, the lord high steward, and the judges at the assize cost the city £12 17s. in 1832, and three years later the city council excused itself from making any more lamprey pies for royalty on the ground that no provision was made for the payment of the royal perquisite under the Municipal Corporations Act.

Queen Victoria, however, got her pie, if a trifle late, for the
custom was revived again in 1893 and continued until the
death of the loyal pastrycook of Westgate Street who baked
the pies. The fame of royal lamprey pies reached the court
and ear of Catherine the Great of Russia and, at her request,
Severn lampreys were caught and sent to her table.

The river flows away from Framilode in a great horseshoe
bend eight miles long round the parish of Arlingham. The
neck of this peninsula is only a mile and a half wide, and
you may watch the Bore at Frampton and walk from here to
Framilode to meet it again, for while the wave takes over
half an hour to sweep round Arlingham, it will take you
twenty-five minutes or less to walk across the peninsula.
There are no less than five churches lying about this neck of
land, all within two miles walk of one another. They are
Framilode, Saul, Whitminster, Frampton, and Fretherne.
The village of Saul takes its name from the French *saule*,
a willow, and was in homelier times known as Salley, which
to this day is a local word for the willow. Though the
church is old, Saul became a parish less than a hundred
years ago and her small houses, which date from the early
Victorian period, have a fantastic ugliness all their own.
They run to every excess of design and ornamentation. All
proudly proclaim the dates of their construction in plaques
built into their façades, but their great virtue is that no two
of them are in the least alike. Saul at this period, owing to the
Gloucester–Berkeley and Severn and Thames canals intersecting
in this village, must have had many a small capitalist with
money to build himself a house and enough to satisfy his extra-
vagance in architectural taste. These little houses have none
of the skimpiness of dingy poverty, they are awful parodies of
the large houses built by the Victorian parvenu. To Saul's
French name might be added that line of La Fontaine: 'Tout
bourgeois veut bâtir comme les grands seigneurs.'

Frampton, by contrast, is perhaps 'the loveliest village of
the plain,' with houses of mellow brick and black-and-white
half timber, which are set off to their best advantage by

Rosamund's Green, a twenty-acre grass lawn in the middle of the village. Fair Rosamund, mistress of Henry II, is reputed to have been born at Frampton, or what was then its hamlet Fretherne, and her name and memory have given abiding beauty to the place of her birth. The green was, however, anything but a blessing to Frampton until it was drained by Richard Clutterbuck two hundred years ago, a work which freed the village from ague, which complaint at that time was very prevalent in the district.

Some fifty years ago Rosamund's Green was the scene of much anger and laughter, when Cole, the landlord of the 'Horseshoes,' played a practical joke on the neighbourhood. He announced that he had a water otter and challenged the dogs of the district to catch it. Not only did poachers come with their lurchers, but quite a number of the more disreputable members of the gentry turned up with their dogs. Rosamund's Green was thronged with dogs and their owners, and spectators came from far and wide to witness a unique sporting event.

Cole, a vast, ponderous man, left the 'Horseshoes' with a sack over his shoulder. He strode over the green and waded into the pond. Out in the middle of the pond he emptied the sack, looked at the crowd, and beat a hasty retreat for home. I do not know whether any one saw the kettle as it left the bag, for it was filled with water and sank like a stone to the bottom of the pond. Every man urged his dog into the water without success and it was not long before someone brought a kettle to the surface. And what is a kettle if not a 'water 'otter'? That is if you drop your 'h's,' as did almost every one in the days of Queen Victoria.

I suppose the disreputable gentry who never dropped an 'h' were the most annoyed, every one was angry, and then the silly joke of the thing dawned on them and they rocked and roared with laughter. Cole had some uncomfortable minutes behind his bar while he had visions of seeing himself dumped along with his 'water 'otter' in the pond. But as soon as he heard the crowd laughing he knew that his little game had worked, for when a man laughs he likes a pot of beer. The 'Horseshoes' was filled with many drinking men, who drowned in floods of beer their disappointment at being defrauded of the expectation of an afternoon's sport. The house has never sold so much beer before or since, and Frampton men over their mugs of cider still laugh over the joke of the century of landlord Cole and his 'water 'otter.'

Fretherne is no more than a hamlet, overshadowed by the court and the church. They are two of the ugliest buildings I know. The church, built in 1847, is the worst example of the worst period in English architecture, blistering the natural beauty of its surroundings by its very ugliness. Traces of the southern thrust of the Ice Age are to be seen in a stony field in this parish, and a sixty-foot cliff, known as the Hock, overlooking the river, contains many fossils.

A battle is supposed to have been fought here between the Britons and the Saxons, when, after their defeat at the battle of Dyrham, the Britons retired to this peninsula of the Severn. Geography lends credence to this apocryphal incident of English history, recorded by William Camden, for what could be more likely than that the Britons, after their defeat at Dyrham, should make for the crossings of the Severn at Priding and Newnham?

On this day Unla Water probably received its name from the Saxons, for Unla is a contraction of the Saxon word for misfortune. Here many a Saxon saw the river for the first time and plunged in only to be drowned. As they saw the Britons running across Priding's Point to the safety of the Silurian shore, it must have seemed a simple matter to the Saxons to cut off this retreat by swimming the narrow main channel of the river. But Unla Water as it runs under the north bank of Arlingham is the most dangerous reach of the Severn and even at low tide is a maze of currents and whirl-pools. Sometimes you see clouds of mud hurrying along in Unla Water, so that you think that they are reflections of real clouds, until you look up and are surprised to see that the sky is cloudless.

VIII. ARLINGHAM

Queen Elizabeth I and her favourite, the Earl of Leicester, came to Arlingham and were entertained at Wick Court. The earl was patron of a hospital at Warwick for the maintenance of men hurt in the wars and, wishing to impress the queen, he extended the scope of this charity to two Arlingham men that the village might ever remember his visit here with Her Majesty.

His foundation continues, but now after four centuries the village looks on his charity as a sour apple, for the name Warwick from time to time spells banishment to ageing hearts in Arlingham. When out of necessity they leave the village for a distant county town, they forsake the broad Severn a mile wide to discover its stripling tributary the Avon, a river fouled by the industrial midlands, bereft of sport, gossip, and small talk. Gone are the bright orchards of the Hesperides which are Arlingham's chief glory. Gone, too, are the cider and perry, a mug of which was within reach of the poorest and gladdened their hearts from boyhood to old age. There are no tides at Warwick to lend dignity to weatherwise conversation over the cups. No one has ever heard of a lave-net or tasted elvers fresh from the frying-pan in the month of March. Age, penury, and infirmity make escape impossible, but more than one rebellious old heart from Arlingham has taken to drink in Warwick and, by bringing temporary disgrace upon his head, he gets 'sent down' from Warwick and in his rustication finds paradise regained in Arlingham. These local patriots return to the village, which receives them with humorous affection. Their temporary exile and return has made them worthies in the parish, and over mugs of cider they give Warwick a worse name in Arlingham than any other town in England enjoys anywhere else in the kingdom.

In order that they might eat their salmon perfectly fresh from the river, the earls of Berkeley sometimes drove over to

78

Wick Court to eat their dinner. The aristocracy has left Arlingham, which is now a village of yeomen farmers, and Wick and the house of Slowwe, pronounced Slough, whose motto was 'Slowwe is Sure,' are now farmhouses. Slowwe is reputed to be haunted by the ghosts of two old ladies, while Arlingham Court has vanished with its phantoms. A phantom funeral was said to be seen coming up the long avenue of trees to the court whenever the head of the house was about to die. This ghost has been laid, for the family has died out, the avenue has been felled, and of the house, which was standing sixty years ago, nothing remains. Only the round dovecote in the field of pasture, known as the Groves, tells that here stood a manor house, and the two cedar-trees in the middle of the field stand as silent reminders of forgotten elegance.

Though the parish is almost moated by the Severn no one makes a living from the river, nor is there a boat in Arlingham. The village, surrounded as it is by fertile farmland, is some distance from the Severn, and Arlingham even buys her elvers from Framilode. Yet there are a few who go fishing with a lave-net, not by the orthodox method of salmon fishermen, but boys and youths who hold a net against the tide. By this means they catch plaice, grey mullet, and other sea fish. The village has never forgotten the fate of one Aldridge, whose family still live in Arlingham, who two hundred years ago was drowned by a flat fish while fishing. Aldridge had caught a plaice and was holding the squirming fish between his teeth, so as to have both hands free for the net, when the fish jumped down Aldridge's throat. Aldridge stood in the river choking until he finally collapsed and drowned.

Corn and grass do their best on the heavy river silt of Arlingham and the parish has thrived under grass as well as under the plough. The great period of Gloucester cheesemaking came to an end in 1840, when the high price of wheat caused Severnside farmers to turn from cheese to bread. They found the change to be a profitable one; Arlingham farmers have harvested eighty bushels to the acre, and one

tenant farmer made as much as £6,000 from his harvests
during the Crimean War. Fifteen years later arable farmers
found themselves facing ruin owing to bad harvests and the
low price of wheat.

Up to the beginning of this century it was the custom for
a band of harvesters to come all the way from Tetbury to
reap the harvest in Arlingham. As the Severnside harvest
began a fortnight earlier, the Cotswold men were able to do
their reaping in Arlingham and return in time for their
commitments on the hills. A band of nine or ten of them
would give up the best part of a day to walk a score of miles
to Arlingham. Their only implements were a reaper's hook
and a stick. Their leader, the eldest of them, was lord of the
harvest and the best reaper of them all. He would open the
field with his sickle and his followers would work in a line
behind him. They received seven shillings an acre, and reaping
from dawn to sundown a man averaged an acre a day. At this
price they earned double and more than double their daily
wage at other times of the year. Is there a man left in
England who can in a day reap an acre of standing wheat
with a hook?

The reapers camped in the open or under the shade of
the great pear trees, possibly a little drunk with the un-
accustomed heady perry, which here took the place of harvest
beer. For their victuals a 'rudge of peas' had been sown
weeks before so as to be ready with the harvest. By such
simple means did men obtain their daily bread when Arlingham
glowed as a land of plenty to Cotswold men.

Only a generation divides the mechanized farming of
to-day from the biblical husbandry as seen on Severnside
into the present century. Old methods have persisted here
longer than elsewhere, and during the last great arable period,
from 1840 to 1879, it was the ox more often than the horse
that drew the plough. On such heavy soil as this the ox has
obvious advantages. Peasant snobbery was, however, responsible for the liberation of the ox from the plough. In
England the horse is still a half-sacred animal, for few will

eat his flesh and his saddle is a worthy throne for a king. When the horse became harnessed to the plough, those who still ploughed with oxen laboured with a sense of social inferiority. Arlingham's last memory of ox-ploughing is of the old man who was punished for goading his oxen, and one may half sympathize with him for the humiliation he suffered in their company.

Arlingham is one of the cider and perry growing villages of the Severn. Her orchards do not lend beauty to the riverside like those of Minsterworth, Longney, and Awre, but that secret vein of blue clay running through Minsterworth and Rodley crosses the river below Framilode to make the cider of Milton End stand out above its neighbour Arlingham's best. The blue line runs out past Hock Cliff to reappear across the Severn in Awre.

Of all earthly possessions there are few to rival a perry orchard beside the river Severn, for a perry orchard will satisfy the spirit of man from boyhood to old age. 'He who plants pears plants for his heirs,' and it takes about as long for a perry orchard to mature as it is said to make an English gentleman, for though signs of grace may be seen in a lifetime it will remain for your grandson to appreciate truly the man you were when he walks beneath the forest giants you planted in the prime of manhood.

Throughout the great cider lands of France, Norman and Breton landscapes have nothing approaching the stature of our Severn pear-trees. A perry orchard is a pleasure to the eye at every season of the year. In midwinter the pear is the shapeliest of trees, superior to the apple in elegance as perry is to cider as a drink. In spring the blossom, canopied fifty to sixty feet against an April sky, presents a sight unmatched in all England, and when the blossom falls no other tree possesses quite such a delicate shade of green. Through summer each tree holds twenty thousand fruits no bigger than your thumb. In autumn the lustre of a myriad fruits is outshone as the leathery leaves change by turn to yellow and red.

The harvesting of such great trees defies the longest ladder

and a man might as well try to pick acorns off an oak. The
pears drop from the trees with the first leaves and provide a
busy week for children, who gather them into sacks, which lie
about the boles of the trees until carted off to the cider mill.
The pear is not so subservient to the soil as the vine, and a
man may drink as he chooses, according as his forebears have
planted. I have drunk Huff Cap at midday and Barlum at
supper, both from the same small orchard, and the contrast
has been as great as that between port and claret. Huff Cap
is a most potent drink and one of these great trees in a good
year will produce enough liquor to lay every man in the
village on his back by Christmas. Barlum is a drink for one
who cares for good liquor; it may be compared with a fine
light wine that you may drink like milk, which like champagne
will make your tongue flow, and you will be surprised to find
that you have drunk more than you thought before the night
is over.

Though the pear and apple are not so sensitive to the soil
as the grape, the right soil is of prime importance in the
making of perry and cider. Inferior soils produce ropey
cider; this term is used for cider that becomes stringy in the
cask. Fouesnant in Brittany grows the best cider in the
world, in a district where bad cider is unknown. The cider
of Fouesnant is so excellent that a small glass of it is more
expensive than wine in the few cafés in Quimper that are
fortunate enough to sell it. A Breton farmer of my acquain-
tance took some young trees from his brother-in-law's orchard
in Fouesnant and planted them in his own orchard a dozen
miles away, but found that when removed from Fouesnant
the trees failed to live up to their ancestry.

The great days of English cider- and perry-making have
declined and much valuable knowledge has perished with the
passing of simple men. Cider-making to-day is a commercial
business on a big scale, or a domestic affair in which the
farmer caters for the thirst of his family and his labourers.
Haphazard orcharding has led to haphazard cider and perry.
An orchard with a dozen varieties of fruit all dedicated to

Photo: P. C. Palmer

the cask are too often crushed together, and many a fine flavour has been lost in a crowd. When the old-fashioned stone cider-mill is used it pays to crush each variety separately, since some varieties require more crushing than others. The machine is not so discriminating and a mass press undoubtedly lowers the standard of the cider in the cask. The farmer, unless he is a cider specialist, cannot be blamed for this, for cider-making is another job in the over-full calendar of the farming year. But a farmer proud of his cider crushes his fruit according to its variety and blends the vatted juices according to his fancy, often mixing cider to perry with rich harmony.

Orchards are the only woodlands of consequence to the east of Severn and here the fox and badger make their earths. Although the badger interferes but little with man's activities and is only guilty of the occasional theft of a solitary chicken, he makes more of a nuisance of himself here than does the fox. He has made his sett in the bank of the drainage rhine leading down to the pill. His delving claws cast hundredweights of earth into the channel and thus he hampers the drainage of the farm. Thirty years and longer have failed to exterminate him or evict him from his chosen lair. In the old days he was dug out, but a good badger digs faster than a man, and always a few survived to carry on the tradition. A new method was found to bolt them from their holes: water was pumped into the setts from the rhine and as the badgers came to the surface from the rising water they were shot. These shyest and most tenacious of animals even survived this calamity. They achieved this by making a fresh tunnel above the rising water level and, sealing its entrance with a quantity of loose earth, they ultimately made their escape by a fresh exit.

Though I count myself lucky if I see a badger once every two years they are common enough in this county, particularly on the hills. Only a field's breadth separates a badger's sett from the sea wall at a point where, a few years ago, a seal found his way over the dyke to surprise a cowman when he came to call in his herd for milking. It must have been a terrible moment for this poor creature when he found himself transported, apparently by his own volition, from the freedom of the seas into the heart of rural England; for no one standing under the high bank of Arlingham's sea wall would suspect that the salt tide was a stone's throw away. The seal lacked either the instinct or the strength to climb back over the sea wall, which is a steep ramp of turf, and even had he done so his bewilderment would have been as great as ever, for the sea that had swept him in would have retreated, leaving a desert of mud and sand. The cowman returned to the village with a strange tale, but milking had to be done and breakfast eaten before the villagers came down to the sea wall only to find that the seal had died, probably through shock at being faced by the terrors of another world.

This sea wall was built by the soldiers of Lord Berkeley's private army during an interlude in the Hundred Years War. A work of fortification for the protection of the realm against the forces of nature and one well suited to soldiers unskilled and indolent at husbandry. This sea wall, though very thick and strong, is not always proof against the Severn at times when the river is brimful under a powerful storm. More than once in a long lifetime Arlingham has known a breach in the sea wall. The last break was forty yards wide when the tide swept up past the lowest cottages as far as the garden gate of West End Farm. The cottagers were marooned and compelled to move upstairs with their pigs and poultry. As there was no boat in Arlingham no one knew how to rescue these cottagers, until the landlord of the New Inn at the passage, seated in his spring cart, drove his mare Kitty into the flood. This brave mare when out of her depth swam dragging the cart behind her until the cottagers were brought to safety.

In former times many travellers passed through Arlingham in order to cross the Severn, for here was the only place where horse and carriage could ford the river between Gloucester and the sea. The position of this ford may still be seen at low tide where the water ripples over the shallow

bed of rock, six hundred yards above the town of Newnham
and a little below the hamlet of Broad Oak. It ceased to be
serviceable in 1802, when the channel of the river altered its
course and removed the bed of sand which joined the rock to
the shore. I have often been tempted to try this ford to discover whether it is passable to-day, but whenever I pass
by here at low water it is invariably the wrong time of the
year for a paddle. This passage was one of considerable
danger as the water is exceptionally deep on either side
of the rock. Samuel Rudder notes that it was used by
'persons of more resolution than prudence,' and adds that
'some have miscarried in the attempt.'

The last person to use this ford was John Smith of Little-
dean when he took the tenancy of Overton Farm, Arlingham.
Changing farm is the greatest event that ever takes place in
the life of a farmer; it requires both courage and determination.
John Smith was a determined man for he took his entire stock
of cattle and sheep, his wagons, his chattels, and his family
without loss over Newnham Passage. His descendants still
farm in Arlingham and who, having farmed here, would wish
to farm anywhere else?

IX. NEWNHAM AND NEW GROUNDS

Newnham is a hill and river town. It belongs to the landscape, which has given it a beauty denied to it by the architect. It is seen at its best from across the river. Here you must descend the bank, steep and sticky with Arlingham's mud, and walk across the yellow sands of the river bed to hail the ferryman. If you are wise you will time your passage for high water; owing to the mud, few people living locally care to make the passage at any other time.

Those living in Newnham and Arlingham make little use of the ferry; I know an Arlingham farmer who has only crossed the passage twice in fifty years, and the town of Newnham has even less need than the village for this amenity. The ferryman, who sometimes does not have a passenger for days, spends his time cobbling shoes so that often the call of the traveller fails at first to rouse him from his last. He is, however, no mere boatman, he belongs to the saintly and infernal tradition of ferrymen. He is as inexorable as Charon and as charitable as St. Christopher. As he rows towards you, you know that there is no escaping him. He answers your good day, but he regards you not as a fellow being but as cargo. No matter what you weigh, though I suppose somewhere he has his limit, he hoists you on to his shoulders, and before you can diffidently protest about your weight he has carried you through the shallows and dumped you in his boat.

He has told me that sometimes his passengers nearly strangle him. I am not surprised; thirteen or fourteen stone of human dignity when swept off its feet does not lightly adapt itself to the posture of helpless infancy.

The ferryman is one of the kindliest of men. I once hurried several miles to the passage so as to catch the bus from Newnham. The ferryman came down to the water, placed three little children in his boat, and took them for a pleasure cruise that lasted for about twenty minutes while I shouted to be carried across. Probably I should have shouted louder and longer, but I felt that it was impolitic to annoy one who had the power to keep me waiting upon his convenience indefinitely. When at last he came, and I told him that I still hoped to catch my bus, he apologized and I forgot my resolve to 'nearly strangle him.'

Were I the ferryman I think that I too would keep my passengers waiting for twenty minutes on sunny summer evenings, for there are few pleasanter places on which to spend an idle half-hour than these yellow sands. Any one waiting at this spot realizes that the position of a town or village is more important than its architecture.

The red of Newnham Cliff is enhanced by clusters of scarlet, pink, and white valerian, a plant which promises to increase on its bare face. There are still a few wallflowers left, which once so clothed the cliff that in the words of the ferryman 'you could come here with a wagon and take a load away and not know that you had been there.' But frosts and rains and occasional landslides have sheared away this annual harvest of spring blooms. Newnham is a town of flowers, for not only are its gardens luxuriant, but the road as it runs through this hill town passes through a valley of grassy banks, which become an unforgettable mass of daffodils in the spring.

More than three hundred years ago the first greenhouse in England was built here by Sir Edward Mansell, there being a small glass-making industry in this place. Sir Edward heated his greenhouse cheaply with local coal brought from the forest on the backs of pack-horses. It would be interesting to know what he grew and what measure of success he achieved. In later years enthusiasm for this greenhouse waned, and a hundred years later only its foundations were to be seen, yet Newnham and Sir Edward Mansell deserve an honoured place in the history of British gardening.

Though the church is modern and two of the most imposing buildings ugly, Newnham is a place in harmony with its surroundings. The churchyard as it towers above the Severn commands the finest panorama of the river, as the silver stream winding in its bed of golden sands, flanked by green meadows, describes the great horseshoe bend round Arlingham. This view may be seen to even better advantage from Pleasant Stile, a mile behind the town, from where the great width of the river makes it unique among English landscapes. Two miles to the north the spire of Westbury church, grey as a heron's wing, marks the village. This greyness is due to the wooden shingles, which form the eight faces of this spire, rising from low eaves to one hundred and sixty feet. The original shingles were cut from the sawn-up staves of cider barrels, in the days when the cider of Westbury-on-Severn was famous, for to quote the poet John Philips, who wrote a long poem in the Miltonic style on cider:

> To the utmost bounds of this
> Wide universe, Silurian cider born,
> Shall please all tastes, and triumph o'er the vine.

Lines which, though written two hundred and fifty years ago, have the masterly touch of modern advertisement. Not that Silurian cider needed any advertisement, for the Styre cider of Westbury-on-Severn sold for as much as fifteen and twenty guineas a hogshead, and was exported from Newnham to London and Dublin. The association between Newnham and Ireland began when Henry II came here to confer with Strongbow about the conquest of Ireland. The town has since shown Ireland's dependence on England by the export of coal, oak-bark for tanning, and cider to Dublin, a trade which continued until the opening of Sharpness Docks.

Styre cider is now no longer a memory, though its name is still associated with Westbury. Fashion lost this extravagant taste, or possibly the Styre apple refused to flourish, for it disappeared from here in the middle of the last century.

Westbury must have been an exciting place in prehistoric times. Some enormous bones were dug up in the village and were believed to be human relics from the time when 'Gomer's giant brood inhabited this isle,' and on this account they were placed in the church. Charles I ordered an inquiry to be made as to their origin, and they were examined by no less a savant than Harvey, the discoverer of the circulation of the blood, who pronounced that they were the bones of elephants, brought to Britain by the Emperor Claudius. They were almost certainly the bones of mammoths, who lived here in the Ice Age, and molars of these great animals have been found at Purton and elsewhere along the Severn.

Though Westbury parish is bounded by eight miles of the Severn, Garden Cliff belongs to the village. It is the most brilliant and impressive of many cliffs rising from Severn shore. At a distance it is bizarre, colourful, and exotic, but you need to walk beneath this precipice to understand its enchantment. It is best reached by Strand Lane, for at this point Garden Cliff is at its highest and most colourful.

The cliff is a vivid red, streaked by two strata of green stone, the colours of a faded Turkey carpet. The cliff may be described in terms of geology, but can only be appreciated as the subject for a painting. Last time I walked beneath the cliff it was a sunny, frosty day in winter. Icicles hung with the beauty of colourless jewels donned for the occasion against the stone almost as old as time. Even the Severn was forgotten, it might have been any water, but the cliff belonged to the ancient glories of Asia, the road to Xanadu, an exultant fragment from Coleridge's vision.

As the cliff loses height so it loses colour, and the red and green tone off with the imperceptible abruptness of the rainbow into buff and grey. It was these buffs and greys that gave Deerhurst its church and chapel, those reds and greens the Romans wove into their tessellated pavements. The cliff awaits a painter with the vision of Cézanne and the boldness of Gauguin, who from some other wall will make reality unbelievable to the eye of the beholder.

Why the cliff is called 'Garden' remains a mystery, unless it is on account of its exceptional colouring, for it is bare of the slightest vegetation, except where the thorn bushes lean over the precipice with mistletoe festooned in their branches.

Forty years ago the cliff was thought to contain gold and may indeed do so, but the tests did not come up to expectations

D

and we may be thankful that the cliff has not been destroyed by the miner. A roadmender, working in Strand Lane, told me that as a child he played with the rock supposed to contain gold, but he countered my curiosity by saying that he did not think that any of it remained. Though I do not look like a mining prospector or company promoter, I like to think that his reticence came from his wish to preserve Garden Cliff from the vandal.

I only know of one salmon taken off Westbury, and that poached by an amateur. The pleasures of poaching are many. There is the capture, the pleasure of not getting caught, the pleasure of swallowing your crime, and not least the pleasure of talking about it when danger of discovery and prosecution is past.

I met an old man in the last of these moods, gathering acorns on Chestnut Hill. He was a retired miner of the Forest of Dean, and when his work in the pits was past he was employed delivering coals by horse and cart to Westbury and other places. It was on a February day that he came with a load of forest coal for the houses at the end of Strand Lane. At the mill he saw a salmon nosing at the sluice gate and, getting down from his cart, he crept into the water and took a place kick at the fish. To any who know the ways of salmon such a feat might seem a tall story, but I suppose that the salmon was so keen on entering the closed gate that it did not have time to turn.

The coalman's kick landed the salmon on the mud of the bank, where he pounced upon it, while a woman from the houses kept shouting: 'Thee 'll go to prison for that,' for there is nothing that annoys a woman more than crimes in which she can have no part and poaching is one of them. But the coalman delivered his coals, wrapped up his fish in a sack, and went home to Cinderford. It is no mean feat to take a sixteen-pound fish out of its element with nothing more than one's physical agility, and this old poacher was rightly proud of what he had done. A fish this size was, however, something of an embarrassment. He kept a pound, for himself, sold a pound or two for a bob a pound, and took the rest to the fishmonger, who retailed it at enormous profit.

It is curious that Severn tide should share with London's river the name of Strand, but, what is even more remarkable, the sands on the opposite bank are known as Pimlico. The cattle from Arlingham's pastures chew the cud on the bare acres of Pimlico, though they are more often to be seen in the river bed below Newnham, where they add much to the beauty of the landscape. They seem to have great prescience about the tide, for the river is so wide at this point that a whole herd might be drowned if surprised by the Bore. The carcasses of animals so often seen in the Bore have been thrown into the tideway by lazy farmers to save the trouble of burial, and a carcass will travel on many tides before it disintegrates.

A craving for salt as much as a surfeit of grass drives the cattle on to the sands where they drink the brackish water of the river. This, in the case of cows, reduces the milk yield, though the farmer does nothing to stop them doing so and the loss of a few gallons of milk is cheaper than putting a fence along the river that a high Bore may destroy. I have often seen Arlingham cows drinking Severn water opposite Ruddle. The manor and fishery of this little hamlet, just below Newnham, were given by Henry I to the abbey of Gloucester so that a wax candle might burn perpetually before the tomb of his elder brother, Robert, Duke of Normandy. If candles were costly, these cast a lurid light on human nature, since Henry kept Robert a prisoner in Cardiff Castle for the best years of his life. Robert still lies in Gloucester Cathedral under his magnificent effigy, carved in bog oak, with his legs crossed to remind one that he could at least look back to his crusading days during his long imprisonment.

Bullo, like Ruddle, has lost its importance. An Elizabethan man-of-war was built in its muddy creak, and with the coming of the railways Bullo Pill superseded Newnham as a port. Newnham had by then lost the cider and oak-bark trade and it remained for Bullo to export the forest coals.

The coal barges often had to wait high and dry on the Arlingham shore for high water. The bargees came ashore at Arlingham where they got drunk. In this state of maudlin inebriety, with money spent and thoughts of hungry families at home, they robbed Arlingham's fields and gardens of fruit and vegetables.

To-day no barges come to Bullo Pill, and the only craft on the water is the small boat of a salmon fisherman. A distant prospect of this fisherman, half a mile away in the midst of the river, is a wonder to behold. The man leaps from the boat, his wide lave-net spread-eagled above his head as he runs across the water. His movement, splashing the water as he goes, is like the prolonged motion of a wild duck while it scuds between swimming and flying. It seems incredible to the eye that a man can run across the middle of a mighty river and only the slight splashing made by his feet shows that he is mortal. He almost seems to be carried by his net, and his movement is one of superb grace, like the climax of a ballet, on a smooth stage surrounded by England's loveliest scenery. The hunting instincts of the animal have come to life within him, giving his simple movements an eagerness that civilized life has almost forgotten. He runs for fifty yards, the water never rising above his ankles, until he turns to plunge the great net from above his head into the water.

At this moment of climax, a relaxation in his body shows that his efforts have been disappointing. There is no silver in his net as he lifts it out of the water into the sunlight, and a salmon shooting upstream has outdistanced him in this river handicap. As he walks back to his boat it is hard to connect this man with the inspiration of his grace of movement, which a few moments ago had filled the landscape with splendour. Yet his boat is still the hub of the landscape, and one knows that among the daily excitements and occupations of men in the plain and on the hills, none has touched the experience that is his. The sight of him running across the water in the centre of the river bed has a blend of fact and fantasy which is the core of poetry.

In absolute contrast to this type of fishing, salmon are caught in baskets along this stretch of river down to the sea. The basket, known as a putcheon or putt, is a wicker funnel five feet six inches long, two feet six inches wide, tapering down to two inches at its end. These putts look like skeletons of baskets, but though loosely woven of hazel and withy are exceedingly strong. When some hundreds of putts have been made they are fastened to a weir of stakes, running at right angles from the river bank out into the bed of the river. The mouth of the putt faces upstream and they are arranged in rows tier above tier. In this position they resemble the cells of a honeycomb, though their function is that of a spider's web.

These weirs, which are often fifty yards long and ten feet high, are completely covered by tide at high water; as the tide ebbs there is a natural tendency for the salmon to swim back to the safety of deeper water. If he swims into a weir of putts he is doomed, for when his head is past the mouth of a basket he is unable to withdraw through his inability to swim backwards. He finds himself in a basket, with plenty of room to wriggle but no means of moving forwards or backwards. The tide is on the ebb, the salmon is left high and dry in the basket, where he dies in a matter of minutes.

This type of fishing is very dependent on the twist of the outgoing tide which is by no means consistent. Out of seven hundred putts seven fish, or one per cent on a tide, is good fishing; fifteen fish, or two per cent, is exceptional, and sometimes the outgoing tide may steer all salmon wide of the putts. Only salmon are caught in these traps owing to the wide weave of the putt, though very rarely small sharks have been taken out of the putts at Awre.

At Awre the river, like a thieving cat, often leaves strange game on its doorstep. In July 1943 a small whale, the first of its kind to be seen in the river for twenty years, was seen off Awre threshing its tail. Lost in these strange surroundings, he went down with the outgoing tide on the sand-bank opposite the second and third putcheon weirs by Church

Rocks, where he died either through exhaustion or lack of water, like a salmon in a putt. Though not thirty yards from the Awre bank he presented a nice problem; he was only a small whale, about twenty feet long, but the current here is very swift. He was floated inshore on the incoming tide and dragged up the mud. He weighed about two tons and exhausted those who pulled him ashore. A man from Blakeney was soon on the scene and cut off a couple of hundred-weight for his pigs, the rest of the carcass was sold to a fell-monger, who carted the animal away in a lorry, cutting off the head and a yard from the tail.

I only saw the mark of the whale where his dead body had carved a channel through the mud. Although only twenty minutes' walk from the village, few villagers saw the whale and even the children preferred to see a plane which crash-landed in the parish the same afternoon.

No photograph was taken of the whale and only two or three people saw it alive. Opinion in the 'Red Hart' was that the creature had been chased from the ocean by its kind, and that only a whale sick unto death would come to die at Awre.

The 'Red Hart' was named after the red deer of the forest, which often came down here to soil themselves in Severn mud or Bream's Pill. The last of our noblest big game in Britain continued here until a century ago, when they were exterminated by order of early Victorian officialdom to remove the temptation of poaching from the Forest of Dean miners. Contemporaries of the last of the red deer were the kite, the buzzard, and the purple emperor butterfly, all of which have since become exterminated through the stupidity and cupidity of man.

The Victorian egg and bird collector did incalculable harm to the rarer species of our birds and butterflies. He was often a wealthy man with the mind of a schoolboy. He would pay the equivalent of a week's wage to the farm labourer who brought him a clutch of eggs of a rare bird. If he was a butterfly collector he would visit the locality of

a rare insect and would catch as many as would fill the
entire length of a drawer in his butterfly cabinet. Many of
these rare insects were caught before they had a chance of
breeding and the adult butterfly collector is alone responsible
for the extinction of the purple emperor in the Forest of
Dean.

Awre is pronounced 'r,' or if you roll your r's 'ah.' The
village has a sad look about it, and with reason, since for
eight hundred years the river has been eating away the land
in this parish. Sternhold was probably born here, and it was
at Awre that he and Hopkins collaborated in their metrical
version of the psalms, but their homes have long since been
swept away into the Severn, and a port called Pomerton once
in this parish has disappeared entirely. In recent years large
portions of pasture land in Awre have been carried away.

Awre has not only lost land, but she has had the mortifica-
tion of seeing this land dissolved in Severn mud, washed up
against the opposite shore in front of Slimbridge. In 1233 Awre
claimed Slimbridge Warth, maintaining that it was ground
swept away from Awre. Slimbridge maintained that this
ground was originally part of the arable and pasture land of
Slimbridge before it had been cast up on Awre. A jury
awarded the land to Slimbridge.

Since those days Slimbridge has grown so fat that it can no
longer see the river, divided as it is from the Severn by two
miles of New Grounds to the detriment of Awre. There is a
tradition that the tide at one time came up to Slimbridge
church, and exceptional spring tides may have continued thus
far until the ramparts of the Gloucester–Berkeley canal acted
as a sea wall against the tide. Part of the churchyard is
fringed by a moat, which originally encircled the old rectory.

Two Slimbridge rectors became bishops in the sixteenth
century. Henry Stokesley, who became Bishop of London
in 1536, was a violent persecutor of protestants. Twenty
years later Owen Oglethorpe, rector of Slimbridge, became
Bishop of Carlisle, in which office he crowned Elizabeth I Queen
of England, but that same year he was deprived of his see,

along with thirteen other bishops, for refusing to comply with the articles of the new reformed Church.

Other rectors of Slimbridge have paid £10 a year to Magdalen College, Oxford, for the choir music on top of Magdalen Tower on May Day. The living is in the gift of the college and no doubt, when this custom originated, it pleased the old wags at Oxford that the Cam should pay this tribute to Oxford, for the river Cam flows through Slimbridge parish and the name of the next village is Cambridge. This Cam, which originally flowed into the Severn, now has the humiliation of feeding the canal. There is plenty of good coarse fishing along this water and lads from Frampton and Slimbridge come here with rod and line to do a bit of patting for eels. A worm is threaded many times with cotton thread and the eel, when he bites this bait, gets the cotton inextricably entangled in his back teeth.

A walk along this canal is a monotonous though pleasant one, and a good gravel path leads all the way from Gloucester to Sharpness. Outside Frampton along the canal bank I have found that unusual plant the yellow balsam. Between the canal and Slimbridge is a piece of ground known as the Patch or Shepherd's Patch, which indicates that this was pasture for sheep when these acres were *pré salé*. Mutton fed on acres watered by the salt tide is superior to South Down grown on its native uplands or even to the mountain-fed mutton of Wales. Severnside farmers, who sometimes kill a sheep for themselves, and local butchers are aware of this, but the great English eating public is ignorant of this virtue. The tide-washed acres of the River Severn should be reserved exclusively for the pasturing of sheep, which should be marketed as such in the interests of better eating.

The New Grounds extending beyond the Patch were probably formed in the sixteenth and early seventeenth centuries, for Charles I by his attorney-general began a suit in the exchequer against Lord Berkeley to obtain this land. But the suit was dropped, since the manor of Berkeley extended into the middle of the river, and a later lord built the wall of stones known as Hock Crib which crosses them.   But far from encroaching on Hock Crib the river has moved further away from the wall.

The grounds became extremely valuable as winter keep, cattle fattened on these pastures sooner than elsewhere, and horses were sent great distances to graze here. This was probably because of the abundance of samphire, which at one time was extensively pickled and made up into a medicine.

The river still holds a lien over New Grounds, for the high tides sweep across its acres, where one may meet with skeins of seaweed at any distance up to a mile from the Severn.

At New Grounds, more than anywhere else along the river, the Severn 'wanders a great way into the neighbouring plains, and then returneth back as a conqueror of the land.'

X. THE ART AND CRAFT OF THE LAVE-NET

New Grounds are often fringed by herons keeping their watch on the river. At this point the Severn is a mile and three-quarters wide, where the main channel of the river flows against Awre and the intervening river bed is filled by Frampton Sands and the Noose. Tese vast sands, each as large as a small parish, are separated by the channel of water running inshore as a backwater from the main stream. This water gives the Noose its name. At low tide on a sunny day these golden sands have the fantastic appearance of desert under a mirage, confused as they are by a labyrinth of shallow pools and channels.

For generations this sandy, watery waste has provided the men of Purton and Gatcombe with a prosperous and exciting livelihood in their sporting pursuit of the salmon by means of a lave-net. The first experience of every lave-net fisherman is of being taken into the river by his father, who for safety sake ties the lad into his boat; for many men and nearly all children, on entering the tidal shallows for the first time, become so giddy that they fall down. The vastness of the river is too much for their vision and, because there is no stationary object on which to focus the eye, dizziness overwhelms them. This is due to the peculiar conditions of the river on an ebb tide, for the water does not ebb evenly or even in the same direction.

The main stream ebbs in gushes at intervals of five minutes, while the many lesser channels, feeding the main stream, gush at intervals of half a minute. These gushes flow with such a force that at times they will swamp a boat, and when a gush enters a pool it creates a backwash, which flows against the tide in a wave two feet high, like a miniature artificial bore. Thus many currents, some of them swiftly moving, pass upstream when the tide is on the ebb. There are two types of wave which flow contrary to the tide; they are known as ruts and races. A rut is caused by swift water running over level sands contrary to the ebb tide, while a race is caused by a swift current flowing through a ten- to twelve-foot channel on an incoming tide. These vagaries of the water bewilder the salmon and aid the fisherman, for it is very difficult to catch a salmon in still water. They also enable the fisherman to drift upstream with the backwater of an ebb tide on a current from eight to ten miles an hour.

If the Severn had a coat of arms one quartering would be the Bore under a full moon, another would be a lave-net with grounded handstaff holding a salmon, for the lave-net is no ordinary fishing-tackle but a noble weapon of great antiquity. It is the last true hunting weapon used in Britain to-day, for with the exception of the netting it is made from carefully selected material, which is grown locally, and is, as a general rule, fashioned by the hunter's own hands. With it he uses his bodily strength, his skill, and his animal cunning against one of the swiftest creatures that swim in that creature's element over a wide field, for rarely is the salmon exhausted in the chase, or brought to bay like the hunted stag by a man-made obstacle. The services of no trained animal are used in hunting this quarry. In the construction and use of the lave-net man has invented an extension of his own bodily frame to catch an agile and powerful creature without bait. This is pure hunting.

The parts of the lave-net are the handstaff, the shoulder, the yoke-board, the rimes, the toes, the head-line, the bosom, and the wings. The net is draped over a frame shaped like the letter Y, whose arms are known as the rimes. These rimes are six feet three inches long and their ends cross a few inches below the head of the handstaff, to which they are joined, one either side, by an iron bolt. These timbers are rounded, the rimes being two inches, the handstaff three inches thick, and are held rigid by the yoke-board, a piece of wood three-quarters of an inch thick, four inches wide, and fifteen inches long. The yoke-board is fastened at right angles to the end of the handstaff, like a minute table perched on one leg. The yoke-board has a two-inch hole in its left side, which holds the left rime where it remains a fixture; at the other end of the board the hole is left half open as a socket. This allows the right rime to be lifted from its socket and placed against its fellow, thus enabling the lave-net to be folded up and carried across the shoulder.

The very greatest care is taken when cutting a rime to leave the butt end of a branch at its furthest end, which is shaped and sized like a thumb and is known as the toe. The rimes are adjusted at such an angle that their toes may slide like a Dutch hoe on the bed of the river, for a toeless rime would stick in the sand and mud. The space between the toes is known as the head-line, across which seven or eight feet of net are stretched. The net drops between the tapering rimes, so that when standing propped against a wall it hangs in a pouch below the yoke-board.

Not only do the rimes have to be specially shaped by nature, but even more care has to be taken in choosing a handstaff. Ash is nearly always selected on account of its strength; elm and holly have been used, but holly for all its strength has been found lacking in toughness. It is not only the kind of timber and its required thickness, but its shape that makes the search for a suitable handstaff a long one. A handstaff has to be straight and yet have a bend in it at the right place, six inches below the yoke-board, so as to rest upon the shoulder in perfect balance. It must be bent and not be crooked, and the bend must not be made with knife or spokeshave and thus undermine its strength. Handstaffs, like salmon fishermen, are born not made. Their shape is caused when a sapling makes two leads and one of them is destroyed. The remaining lead, which has begun to bend outwards, shifts its growth to its original vertical position. This is how the handstaff grows its shoulder, and fishermen will ramble as far as a dozen miles from Purton, through copse and spinny, to cut themselves a suitable handstaff. A short man cuts himself a four-foot handstaff, a tall man allows himself another six inches.

LAVE-NET FISHERMAN WITH OPEN NET

FISHERMEN WITH FOLDED LAVE-NETS

A handstaff must have the balance of an oar where its shoulder fits the human shoulder that carries it. Without it the open lave-net would be a clumsy burden, and lightness is essential when a fisherman has to sprint a hundred yards to intercept a racing fish. This consideration of weight is so important that of the dozens of varieties of native willow the black salley, whenever possible, is chosen for the rimes. This willow, which is none too common, combines exceptional toughness with extreme lightness. Poles growing from the ground are invariably selected, since tree timber proves to be too brittle. Even the size of the mesh is considered when studying the problem of weight. By the laws of salmon-fishing no lave-net may have a mesh of less than four inches, but a wider mesh is often used for the sake of lightness. Mesh is measured by taking the opposite corners of a square of netting and extending them to their greatest length. Thus a four-inch mesh is to the eye netting two inches by two inches. The net is knit from a two-pound ball of three-strand Italian hemp twine and is begun from the head-line in a row of fifty-six meshes. Another mesh is added to each row for fifteen rows. Then another three feet are knit into the width of the net, after which the meshes are decreased, until after nine feet six inches of knitting, or nine feet if the fisherman is on the short side, the width is reduced to thirty meshes. The net is now the shape of a giant horseshoe. The bottom of the net is known in the eloquent parlance of fishermen as the bosom, and the sides, most appropriately, when one considers with what speed the fisherman runs with the net above his head, as the wings. The net is fastened to the rimes by a cord, twenty-two feet long, threaded through each mesh; this gives tautness to the head-line and shape to the wings.

A lave-net is all that the salmon fisherman needs for landing the largest fish in Severn, but if he is to catch a lot of fish a boat is also essential. A salmon-boat has been evolved through centuries of experience. It is light, strong, and peculiarly suited to the extraordinary behaviour of the River Severn and that of its fishermen. A typical salmon-boat is

about twelve to thirteen feet long and five feet in the beam,
built of larch on oak timbers.   As in the course of fishing a
boat is often stranded, it must be light enough to be carried
by two men without undue strain.   A keel five inches wide
gives backbone to the boat and enables it to be launched the
easier on mud.   This keel tapers to a four-inch pick-up or
curved bow and stern.   The hull is clinker-built with copper
fastenings.   The general appearance of the craft is rather full
at the stern and fine at the bow.   A full stern prevents the
boat from sucking when anchored in a strong current.   There
are few things that irritate a fisherman more than a boat
that sucks.   When he is wading upstream a sucking boat
drags and throws a heavy wake, which spoils good fishing
when the weather is calm.

The stern of the boat is to the fisherman what the bridge
is to the captain of a ship, for he stands there to get a better
view of any fish in the offing, and a full stern helps to support his weight and preserve his balance.   At other times
he will have to crouch in the stern to prevent his boat from
being wrecked and the bow from being pulled under by a
strong current, for a rut or a race will easily lift up the stern
of an unweighted boat and cause it to run across the tide and
roll over.   These tides are so strong that only the old-fashioned
sailing-ship type of anchor is good enough to hold one of these
small boats, and no Severn man, if he is wise, will look at any
fancy type of anchor.

The boat is propelled by a stout pair of ash oars and sometimes a sail.   But a sail involves the fixing of a centre keel,
and this is a somewhat fragile accessory on shallow fast-moving
water.   The ideal salmon-boat will float in as little as five
inches of water, and with no depth of keel is incapable of
sailing into the wind.   Thus speed and ease of movement are
sacrificed for greater manœuvrability and an aptitude for
facing any unexpected emergency.

Lave-net fishing is an hereditary occupation, and there are
fishermen who, to their certain knowledge, are the sixth
generation in their family to carry a lave-net; and some have

as many centuries of inherited skill bred into their bones. A good fisherman is born not made, and much river knowledge has been handed down like an heirloom from father to son, for these river secrets are jealously guarded and a salmon fisherman will never tell the truth if he can help it.

The use of a lave-net demands speed in action, quickness of eye, and the instinctive judgment of the hunter. The first-class fisherman must have the speed of a rugger three-quarter, the eye of a county cricketer, and must know every yard of the river bed. In this exacting calling a fisherman is past his best at the age of thirty, for he has lost that turn of speed which may make the difference between laving and losing a fish. After thirty, cunning and experience have their day, and many a fisherman when past his prime has another forty seasons ahead of him, and salmon have even been laved by men of eighty.

Few other than fishermen see the Severn salmon in his natural state as he comes up-river volted with the pent-up energy of the sea. He is among the nimblest fish that swim. Over a short distance his speed has been estimated at forty-seven miles an hour. Against a five-mile river current he will outdistance the fastest sprinter with a lave-net over a hundred yards, leaving him sixty yards behind. Yet over twice that distance the salmon may be overtaken and captured.

A salmon swims close to the surface along this part of the river, and he is fished for in shallow water and taken in from two feet to as little as six inches of stream. As he swims near the surface he throws a loom on the water, which the fisherman runs to intercept. Seldom, if ever, is the salmon taken on the incoming tide, but as the tide ebbs it forms shallow sand bars, which run in long diagonal ribbons across the main stream. The salmon drift downstream on the out-going tide, and as the Severn empties with unprecedented rapidity on the ebb, the salmon, with his habit of swimming near the surface, little realizes that there is a danger of his being grounded until he is in very shallow water. He becomes alarmed and instinctively dashes upstream in search of deeper water. His instinct is right, for he cannot hope with all his speed to overtake or keep pace with the emptying tide, furthermore he knows in the course of nature that it is his duty to reach fresh water. Here again his instinct is unerring, for above Framilode there is a depth of water in which he may swim without peril of grounding as far as the slopes of Plynlimon.

He knows, too, that even with the tide at its lowest ebb there is a safe passage, if precarious in places, up the main stream of the river. It is, however, no easy matter, even if he has been spawned in Severn and descended seawards as a pink, to be certain of the way upstream.

He dashes for deeper water and as he does so his movement is seen by the lave-net fisherman. The man of experience knows the line of water that the fish is taking and he knows the bed of the river. He chases the mark without seeing the fish. The fisherman's eye is so used to the surface of the water that he can tell on a moving tide how deep it is and even what obstructions lie beneath it. He also knows that where the water is flowing swiftly, the sand will be as hard as a road to his feet, as though it had been rolled by a roller. It is here that knowledge counts and a novice might easily plunge up to his neck or deeper in a standing pool, or find himself bogged in a quicksand.

The fisherman must get himself in front of the moving mark with five seconds to spare in which to flick the lave-net from his shoulder into the water. In a river as wide as the Severn, the salmon stands a very good chance even against a nine-foot head-line. Here the fisherman's judgment comes into play, for he must move and place himself like a cricketer who sprints to catch a ball heading for a boundary. He plunges the lave-net into the water, so that the toes rest on the bed of the stream. The salmon shoots towards him, but is unable to see him for his eyes stare sideways out of his head, nor in the turbid outgoing tide can the fisherman see the salmon. He waits until the salmon is nine inches from the head-line and then lifts the net. To do this he shovels the net forwards with a lift similar to that of a man shovelling coals.

Every fisherman takes a great pride in the manner in which he laves his fish, and the timing of a perfect lave is when he sees the salmon's tail flick above the head-line as he raises the net from the water.

There are heroes among netted fish who live to swim away. Powerful fifty-pounders, shooting with all the speed and strength in their bodies, sometimes go through a net like a torpedo, leaving the fisherman with a wasted day, and evidence for another story of the fish that got away, and a resolve to get a stronger mesh.

Once the fish is in the net the fisherman grounds the hand-staff by driving his end of the net into the sand. He does this to have a free hand with which to kill the fish. With his right hand he steadies the net, with his left hand he draws the knocker from the inner pocket of his oilskin jacket. The knocker is a truncheon nine inches long, usually loaded with a slug of lead, with a thong to prevent it slipping from wet hands into the water. The fish is then finished off with two or three blows over the head between the eyes.

A salmon will die out of the water in a few minutes and a fish though still living will not revive even when put back into the water five minutes after it has been landed. But apart from the kindness in killing the fish as quickly as possible fishermen are loath to waste time on a good tide.

The salmon is taken from the net, and a light cord, pushed under his gills and out of his mouth, is fastened with a fisherman's knot. The loose end of the cord is then slipped with a double half-hitch around his tail. In this position, the dead fish, hanging like a silver crescent, is slung over the right shoulder until such time as it is convenient for the fisherman to regain his boat, which by now may be half a mile away.

If the fisherman misses his fish he will pursue it and overtake it, unless a more advantageous mark catches his eye. Sometimes in his boat he sees a fish in baulk, a salmon swimming in deep water. In this position the fish is safe from capture, for the fisherman is unable to use his net unless his feet are on the river bed.

In the heyday of salmon fishing, which is still green in the memory of Purton men, eighty men left the village daily to fish in Severn and were joined by others from Gatcombe, and many clashes occurred between fishermen. Two men would often see the same loom, and with their eyes intent on the mark neither would notice the other running until he was well on his way.

This gave mighty zest to the pursuit, nets would become entangled and blows exchanged. This caused great enmity in the river between certain men, for lave-net fishing, apart from being their daily bread, is a great sport and in these clashes a young man's pride in his physical prowess was often at stake. But strangely enough these men, whose tempers rose as quickly as Severn's tides against each other in the river, were the best of friends on shore, and simple good natures readjusted themselves as soon as they set foot on Purton Green.

In the words of one of them, recalling the cunning of man against man when after the same fish: 'A game of chess isn't in it in the river.'

XI. SALMON, SHARK, AND STURGEON

In January the fishermen watch the river for the marks of salmon, which are as clear to their eyes as birds in a meadow, and from the marks they see they can foretell how good or how lean a season's salmon fishing lies ahead of them. On 2nd February the lave-net season opens, the most unpleasant time of the season, but the best for catching fish, for 'February fill-dyke' flushes the river with freshes drained from the flooded meadows of the midlands. This helps to dilute the pollution of drainage from urban areas.

The ideal fishing weather is February or early March with a sharp north-east wind, for a salmon will always head into the wind. And with the wind in this quarter he faces the lave-net on an ebbing tide. Salmon swim close enough to the surface to be conscious of the wind, and they head into the wind for comfort as a seagull rides into the gale, or a boat finds comparative stability by driving into the wind in a storm. A salmon's knowledge of the wind is prophetic and uncanny, for he will anticipate a change of wind by heading towards the quarter from which it is about to blow. It is extraordinary that a creature should be so knowledgeable about an element with which it has no contact, and that such an element should control its movements.

Salmon swim so close to the surface in this part of the river that when driven by fear they will sometimes skim through the shallows with their backs out of the water, and will in this manner become grounded on the gently shelving sands of Severn. More often fish become forsaken by the tide and quickly die, like travellers lost in the desert. These stranded fish the law classes as carrion and they are the property of whoever finds one, wherever it is found. Not every fish that is carrion has died this strange death, some are choked by sand in the gills, and some die of pollution in the higher river and are swept downstream until left by the receding tide. There is a simple and infallible test for distinguishing a 'drowned' fish from one that has been poisoned: a poisoned fish will always float, while a 'drowned' fish, even when stinking, will sink.

In the past carrion has been a most valuable perquisite to all and sundry, and even to-day with the scarcity of fish in the river, on the average a carrion salmon a week is carried ashore at Purton.

As the salmon season draws to its close and the weather improves, Purton fishermen travel immense distances and even continue fishing out as far as English Stones, which is in the estuary, beyond the Severn proper, some twenty-two miles from home. But only on calm days at the beginning of August are they able to risk their boats on such rough and treacherous water, and Gatcombe stopping-boats, built on lines like the lifeboat, are more suited for such ventures.

Towards the end of August the quality of salmon markedly deteriorates. Indeed, after midsummer the gourmet may notice that salmon does not taste quite as good as it did a month or so earlier, and the change is not due to his jaded palate.

The salmon enter the river to spawn and by the end of summer a biological change takes place in the fish, before the spawning season, which lasts from October to January. Fishermen notice that a salmon becomes more of a handful in the net and shows more fight as the water becomes warmer. This is due to the sexual change in the fish, for the salmon is no lover of warm water. Indeed in times of exceptional heat, 'once in a green moon,' as an old Severn man once put it to me, salmon are overcome by the heat, and in the higher reaches of the river, where the water is deep, the fish have risen to the surface where they have 'waddled' in an almost helpless state. In this condition even large fish have been taken by hand, and there is a popular belief that once the temperature of the water exceeds that of the blood-heat of the fish, the fish will die.

Severn salmon spawn far above the tidal reaches of the river, and higher up the river there is a tendency for the cock and hen fish to be seen swimming in pairs.

The Teme and the main stream of the Severn in Mont-gomeryshire are the river's spawning-grounds. But in the Wye the fish are known to spawn within four miles of that river's source on the slopes of Plynlimon, where there is barely enough water to cover their backs. The fish seek the gravelly parts of the river and with their bodies they carve a channel in the river-bed. Here the hen lays her eggs, which are covered and fertilized by the cock fish.

After the salmon season is closed, a fisherman who sees a stranded hen fish in danger of her life through grounding will make great efforts to help her to find deep water and gain her breeding ground.

A fish in spawn is known as a kilt and is spoken of by fishermen as an unclean fish, and as such will not be touched by the most ardent salmon poacher. Nature has preserved the most delectable of fish from man's appetite by making the salmon uneatable in the spawning season. In narrow hillside streams such fish could be taken by the most in-experienced poacher, for after spawning the fish is exhausted, yet no man takes an unclean fish twice. The scales are hard, the flesh is grey and tasteless and sticks to the fork like glue. An unclean fish returns to the sea to renew its vital forces, for the salmon hardly feeds in the river. Indeed, the only food it takes is by suction through its gills; this nourishment is known as the clog and is so minute that the contents of a salmon's stomach could pass through a salt-sifter. Some fishermen maintain that the salmon eats nothing while in the river, others aver that Severn salmon is richer than those taken in Scottish or Irish waters, because those streams are of clearer water, and the clog being less nutritious produces a drier fish.

The experienced eye can recognize the mark of a fish that has spawned. On its return journey it throws a smaller mark and its movements are lethargic. It has lost its salmon-like rotundity and is shrunk to the proportions of a giant herring. Fish that shot up-river as twenty-pounders return mere shadows of their former selves, and are dwindled to nine pounds of skin and bone. Nature must have given the salmon a philosophy and a sense of faith and optimism, for these unclean fish meet the new fish, which have already entered the river from the sea.

It is a great day in a boy's life when he enters the river alone for the first time.

Colin Cooke has told me how he went into the river alone for the first time on a winter's evening, when he saw a gull through the fog pecking at a dead salmon. Lest he should lose himself in the fog, his father stood on the bank hammering his boat with a rowlock to give the lad his bearings, for this sound is heard at a great distance. The fish when he reached it was reddish and dark sooty-green, for it was an unclean fish stranded by the tide on its return to the sea. But the boy carried it triumphantly homewards on his back, until he came across a new fish, left high and dry by the tide, lying like a bar of silver. His first fish was in Colin's eyes the greater prize; he carried the useless kilt on his back, dragging the new fish behind him as he went. On meeting his father he was soundly scolded for the way he had treated the new fish by rubbing off its scales.

A new fish taken in winter is a salmon in prime condition, and because it is taken out of season may not be sold; for this reason there is no greater epicure of salmon than the Severn fisherman. In the days when salmon were plentiful in many fishermen's homes they 'ate salmon like bread,' yet the greatest care was taken in preparing and cooking the fish. The body was washed of slime, but the scales were left on as scaling removes the natural grease of the fish. The stomach was taken out through the throat and the fish steamed whole in a tin bath. The shoulders of the fish are more esteemed than any middle cut, since the finest flavour is found behind the gills. But the greatest delicacy of all, and one which is ignored by the general public, is a piece of flesh behind the eye, shaped like an oyster-shell, and the 'oyster' is greatly enjoyed by gourmets among salmon fishermen.

The earliest record I know of a new fish taken in the Severn was of one poached on 11th November, five or six weeks after the opening of the spawning season, and though the law was doubly broken, the law of nature was not violated, since this fish was not to spawn until the following autumn.

The five ages of salmon may best be explained by quoting from the manuscript notes of Dr. Jenner of Berkeley:

'They are called salmon pinks from the smallest size to a pound weight, a swing from that size to four pounds, a botcher four to eight pounds, from that to sixteen a gilleon, from that to the greatest growth of the fish, a salmon.'

For this reason salmon, irrespective of their size, are nearly always referred to as fish by salmon fishermen. A swing is rarely, if ever, seen in the river, and some contend that the botcher is sexually mature and enters the river to breed.

The pink has a number of natural enemies. He is small fry for eels and pikes, sometimes he is an unwitting victim in an elver-net, and though the elverer is supposed to throw the pink back into the river it is not always easy to disentangle him from a mass of squirming elvers. Thus many a salmon is lost to the net, the putcheon, and the spawning-ground.

As an adult fish he has no enemies except the otter and man. Many a man who has worked all his life within half a mile of the river, and to whom the river is a matter of constant interest, will tell you that he has never seen an otter or that he saw one a few years back. Yet the otter is a common enough animal on the river, and though I very rarely see one I meet his spoor in the fresh mud left by last tide about as often as I see a kingfisher. He makes his holt up pills out of the tide's way and prefers the Gloucester–Berkeley canal to the open vastness of the river bed, which fails to give his retiring nature adequate water cover.

The otter is not a fastidious eater and salmon are not his especial fancy. An amateur naturalist in the last century estimated that otters took seventy Severn salmon in a good salmon year. It would take a small army of trained and experienced observers watching day and night to disprove this arm-chair guess.

The fox makes full use of the tidal river, which he scavenges like a jackal, for his pad-marks in mud and sand show that he nightly patrols the high-tide mark with the regularity of a village constable on his beat.   He does so to see if he can find a wounded wild fowl, and will even dine off a stranded salmon, and the interruption of his pad-marks sometimes show where he has dined too well and vomited a surfeit of fish.

Early one August morning, drifting in his boat upstream on the back current of an ebb tide, Colin Cooke was the solitary witness of an extraordinary co-operation among foxes.   A fox cub was hunting a rabbit on the sand beneath Royal Drift. On a ledge of the cliff four feet above the tide were three other fox cubs, who had spaced themselves four or five yards apart, and from this position they closed in on the rabbit every time he made a bolt for his hole on top of the cliff. They behaved like well-trained sheep-dogs while aiding their brother to bring down his quarry.   Wild animals have little or no fear of a drifting boat, which is an ideal observation post, but unfortunately on this occasion the current carried the boat upstream before the final scene of animal co-operation could be witnessed.

The domestic cat is too canny, or dislikes the mud too much, to venture into the river, but Purton cats have from time to time been seen fishing on their own account in the canal. They have probably watched small boys tiddling for fish. At mating-time the fish come into the reeds to lay their eggs, while lads lying on their bellies dangle their hands in the water and twiddle their fingers until they feel a fish within their grasp.   The cat sits on a tuft of grass by the water's edge, until he sees a fish kicking within striking distance and lands it with a blow from his paw.

The salmon's natural enemy is the fisherman, but fishing, skill, and cunning are outplayed by the common enemy of fish and fishermen, the pollution of the river.   A number of reasons may be given for the river having become polluted to the decrease in the numbers of salmon and the decline of salmon fishing.   Improved drainage, which may satisfy sanitary engineers, fouls the river. Oil from motor-barges between Gloucester and the midlands has discouraged salmon from fighting their way up to the old spawning-grounds, and the tradition of spawning in the Teme and along the reaches of the Welsh river is lost to many of them. Chemical waste from midland factories, irresponsibly swilled into the river, has resulted in the death of many fish, particularly pinks. But perhaps most significant of all, the quality of Severn mud has altered. 'Thirty years ago when I was a child,' a salmon fisherman said to me, 'I wallowed in mud, it was absolutely clean, it was washed soil; to-day it smells.'

As long ago as 1890 fish became noticeably fewer, but what fish there were, were considerably larger. Gloucester sewers were rightly blamed for this loss to fishing. Some idea of past plenty may be gleaned from Samuel Rudder who, writing in 1770, tells us that £4,000 worth of Severn salmon was sent annually to London, the price at that time being fourpence a pound. This represented only a fraction of the amount of fish taken, since quantities must have been sent to Bristol, Bath, and the many smaller towns and great houses within a day's journey of the river. One may wonder how, before the days of railways, this great amount of fish was transported to London before it turned bad. Possibly this trade was restricted to the colder months of February and March, when ice was available to keep the fish fresh on their hundred-mile journey.

Despite the falling off of fish noted in 1890, seven years later, in the year of Queen Victoria's diamond jubilee, half a ton of fish was caught in a day by the stopping-boats in Wellhouse Bay, a mile below Purton on the opposite bank of the river. And immense catches of fish were taken in the bumper summers of 1912 and 1913.

In 1926 there were enough fish in the Severn to be a valuable standby to the Forest of Dean miners during the general strike. A number of them armed with lave-nets tried their luck in the river. They stood in a line across the main stream, their lave-nets toe to toe, to take what fish came to their nets, but even then many a fish skimmed past them upstream to be laved by the professional fishermen. Any fisherman knows that even with the lave-net, the long-net, and the putcheon it is impossible to fish the river clean of fish, for the river is constantly being replenished from the sea. He knows, too, that more fish get by on a flood tide and in the watches of the night than will ever fall to his net, and the number of eggs a hen salmon spawns is enormous.

But if the river water is made unhealthy for fish, the fish will seek sweeter water. We have no means of knowing whether a salmon returns to the river in which it was spawned. This may well be so, and the infant mortality rate among pinks, owing to chemical pollution, most probably accounts for the decline in population among adult Severn salmon.

To-day barely a score of men earn a living with a lave-net the length of Severn tide; a generation ago they might have been counted in their hundreds. There are still, however, a few casuals who wander out over the sands with a lave-net over their shoulder; in the same way that a farmer potters about with a gun when he has an evening to spare. Lave-net fishing is a great sport, and possibly only snobbery has prevented the athletic gentry from trying their hand at this manly and exciting exercise, which fits into the calendar between the end of the fox-hunting and the beginning of the cub-hunting season.

The older salmon fishermen feel that they and the river have had their best days. The grand river feuds are not forgotten, but they belong to the past. Elderly men in their cottage gardens take life philosophically and feel that the river will pass the next generation by, and that their store of river knowledge will perish with them.

A salmon fisherman lives by snatching a prize from nature, and his bond with nature differs from that of the man ploughing on the hill a mile away, for though they move under the same sky they move on different elements. He lives in danger, while chasing a lively fish, of plunging into deep river pools of which there are many in the river-bed. Yet this he seldom if ever does, and most fishermen strangely enough are unable to swim a stroke. You are more likely to escape death from drowning, if you get your living from the lower Severn, by being a non-swimmer than an indifferent one, for, so dangerous are the rapids and currents, and the almost unheralded approach of a Bore tide, that any one buoyed up by the uncertain confidence of a swimmer is more likely to be overwhelmed than the man who only knows the feel of the river-bed under his two feet and whose mind is consequently apprehensive of daily dangers. In his peculiar relationship with nature, the Severn fisherman is more superstitious than the average countryman.

These superstitions are the outcome of several strange coincidences, or may be of deeper significance, for the river breeds individualistic, imaginative men. Seals in the river are regarded by many fishermen with a dread akin to that with which Coleridge's Ancient Mariner regarded the albatross.

Within living memory active men have taken and killed seals, and have soon afterwards been overtaken by unexpected death. A fisherman who accidentally takes a young seal in his net will be quick to release him, for even if he is not a superstitious man, village gossip will cause him sleepless nights.

On the whole the river has been very generous to Severn men and the lave-net has enabled the majority of Purton fishermen to own the house in which they live. A state of affairs which is unusual in an English village, and though Purton is part of the great manor of Berkeley, this has been made possible because the greater part of the village, including the church, stands on what until the last century was common land.

A Purton man, aged forty, has spoken to me with indignation in his voice of how as a boy with other lads at play he was driven off land by a farmer with a whip, and how this land in his mother's childhood had been common ground, which has surreptitiously been encroached upon and enclosed. Possibly the village had been too preoccupied by fishing to take much heed of the hedge which had been set about their common heritage.

There are two orders of fishermen, public fishermen and private fishermen. Both consider themselves superior to the other and great enmity and rivalry exists between them. A public fisherman fishes for himself, a private fisherman is one who owns or leases a private fishery and the men he employs on salary are also private fishermen. Generally speaking the public fisherman has the right to fish wherever the tide flows, the private fisherman is, or is employed by, the riparian owner, who owns half the river against which his land is situated, but does not own the tideway. This distinction and the volatile nature of fish have led to many a legal argument, which has ended in blows for want of a judge.

Fishermen are natural poachers and born lawyers. Colin Cooke has told me how his father, through a poaching escapade at the age of twelve, graduated into a private fisherman.

Young George Cooke decided to go 'groping.' To do this he had to jump school and steal the best carving-fork out of the kitchen drawer when mother was not looking. He tied the fork to a five-foot pole, got hold of a bag, or failing that he used his pocket, and when nobody was about he crept down to the river. If George was safe from the eye of the schoolmaster, he might still be seen by father as he waded through muddy water, but he spent happy hours, poking under rocks for eels and flat-fish, until his day seemed complete when he saw a salmon in a pool. He had already jumped school and taken the best carving-fork, and was not going to pass the salmon by. He groped him with one swift stab, with all the skill of an experienced poacher. But the glory of the day vanished with a voice of thunder from the river bank. It was not father nor the schoolmaster but the water-bailiff. Any one but a water-bailiff would have been speechless with wonder at the sight of a child groping a large and nimble salmon with a carving-fork. But water-bailiffs are not impressionable men. They are the gamekeepers of the river, who keep a watchful eye on fishermen to see that no fish are taken from the river without a licence. Not only had young George taken a fish without a licence, but this fish had been groped in a private fishery.

No one in Purton takes a hard view of a poacher, but to be caught is a different matter. Young George's jumping school and stealing the carving-fork were now trivial offences, he had committed a man's crime, and, when the owner of the fishery threatened to prosecute the young poacher, the situation was decidedly unpleasant.

Old George, the boy's father, was a wise and politic man. He went to the owner of the fishery, apologized for his son's behaviour, and added that the lad's offence showed that he had the makings of a sound fisherman. He suggested that the would-be prosecutor might do worse than drop the charge, buy the lad a licence, and employ him as a lave-net fisherman in the fishery he had poached. By this means the case was settled out of court, and young George began his career as a private fisherman which lasted for over half a century.

It is hard to understand why the Great Western Railway should have bought out Purton Passage, for the sake of a few local fares, and imposed an inconvenience on the people living in Purton and Gatcombe wishing to cross the river. When the passage was closed the road leading down to the slipway two hundred yards further on became grassed over and a gate was put across the road to keep the cattle in. This public right of way was in danger of becoming lost and forgotten, and its importance was by no means negligible, since not only did it give free access to the river, but this is the only point between Framilode and the sea where the river may be crossed on foot at low tide. This crossing is something of a maze and is only known to fishermen who have crossed the river at ankle depth. Old George Cooke for over sixty years from early manhood to extreme old age (he lived to be over ninety) once a year maintained this right of way.

One day in each year he harnessed his pony to his cart, drove up to the gate and demanded of the farmer that he should open it, he then requested him to open the second gate, for there are two gates between Tites Point and the slipway. On reaching the river bank old George drove home and unharnessed his pony.

It takes a steadfast and far-seeing mind to carry out such a simple and lonely ceremony for over sixty years; but actions like this give real meaning to law and constitution. If there had been one man of old George Cooke's character in every English village throughout the last three hundred years the face of England would be unrecognizable to us as we know it to-day. But only men who are born free, as men to a great river are born free, would have got as far as harnessing the horse to the cart.

The eldest George Cooke had the fondness of a Plantagenet king for a lamprey. And like those royal autocrats, not only did he demand every lamprey caught at Purton for his own table, but like Henry III he fixed the price he paid for his fish; he never paid more or less than half a crown.

To any fisherman he saw with a lamprey he would say: 'Come here, that's mine and here's thee half a crown.'

Lampreys are not often eaten in cottage kitchens because wives and mothers don't like the look of the things and don't know how to cook them.

A lamprey cannot be skinned, and George Cooke's lampreys were prepared by scalding the fish and cutting away the gills. The body was stuffed and baked in a covered tin, gently for two hours. The flavour of the fish on the table is not unlike that of a dish of elvers.

The lamprey is a lazy swimmer, but when chasing flat-fish he has a surprising turn of speed. He is the weasel of the river, for he catches on to flounders and dabs to suck their blood and travels up-river in the process. His appearance is as unpleasant as his nature, for he is shaped like an eel with a fin at the top of his tail and is piebald, black and yellow. As he swims close to the surface the mark he throws is some-times mistaken by the fisherman for that of the botcher. He would easily pass through the mesh of the lave-net, if the fisherman did not wrap the grounded net around his slimy body. The only other small fish netted in this way is the twait, which throws a loom similar to that of the botcher.

At the other end of the scale large and unusual fish come to the lave-net, and among sea mammals the porpoise has been taken and eaten at Purton. Its flavour has been described to me by one who dined off it as 'fishy beef' and not to be tasted a second time; yet in the Middle Ages this flesh was valued, and Tidenham sent six porpoises from the Severn every year to Bath Abbey. No doubt in winter when fresh beef was unobtainable fishy beef was not to be despised.

In winter a salmon-net is often taken from its frame, which is decked with a shrimping-net of finer, stronger mesh, for there are plenty of shrimps in this part of the river. Colin Cooke was shrimping out of the salmon season in 1921 when he went for what he thought was a porpoise, a creature with a turn of speed and one that would tempt the eye of any young fisherman. On laving he found that he had caught a tope shark. The water-bailiff, too, thought that he had a catch for he had watched this manœuvre, suspiciously like the taking of a salmon. The photograph of Colin standing beside this shark, in which the fish is hanging from a hook, shows that he was as long as the man is tall, an inch or so short of six feet.

Colin was prouder of his sturgeon than this useless curiosity, for no Purton man is considered complete master of the lave-net unless he has landed one of these royal fish. This is no easy honour to come by, as Colin said to me: 'There have been only two sturgeons taken in my time, and I 'm happy to say I caught one of them.' This sturgeon was about ten feet long and weighed two hundred and forty pounds, and it would seem impossible to catch so huge a fish in a lave-net were not an interesting technique employed. The sturgeon is a fish that hangs about the rocks and is a slow swimmer, and were he as quick as the salmon it is doubtful if ever he could be taken in a lave-net. In addition his great weight, from three to five times as heavy as the largest salmon, would prevent the strongest fisherman from laving the net or grounding the handstaff. With the salmon the fisherman places the net in such a way that the fish shoots towards and under the yoke-board. With a sturgeon the net is placed at an angle so that the fish slides over the head-line and strikes the net in the upper part of the wing, a foot or so below the toe of the rime. His head is now under one rime with his tail still free. The fisherman very quickly swings the net so that the tail is caught under the other rime without loosing his hold on the head. This is the height of perfection in the use of the lave-net. A monster of the river has been trapped without an inch to spare. The skill is all the greater since the fisherman is unpractised, save in his imagination, in the quick deft strokes he employs. He is lucky if the chance comes his way once in a lifetime. The sturgeon, secured under the rimes, is floated to the shallows where the help of several strong men is needed to drag him ashore. Of all river fish, with the exception of the eel, the sturgeon is the most tenacious of life. He is said to be a survival from some biological period in the world's prehistory and when landed he lives up to this reputation. He has a head like stone, which defies the strongest arm with a knocker, nor will he readily die after the manner of most fish on dry land, but will live for twelve hours or longer out of his element.

I have never heard of caviare being made or taken from any Severn sturgeon, and the methods employed by the fishermen on the Volga and Danube would be distasteful to Severn men. The flesh of the sturgeon is reputed to have the flavours of fish, flesh, and fowl and the origin of sturgeon as 'royal fish' is lost in obscurity. No doubt its very size required that it should be reserved for royal banquets, in times when to eat royally was to eat enormously. Kings in the past no doubt have had their fun with the fish, when, the queen or some lovely mistress having refused a second helping of fish from the royal hand, the lady has been offered a helping of fowl, and after eating her fowl and refusing more has been cajoled to eat her portion of flesh.

The Severn, Britain's greatest sturgeon river, was a long way from court, except at such times as the Norman kings, and one early Plantagenet, held court in Gloucester, as did William the Conqueror, William Rufus, Henry I, and Henry III.

A sturgeon could not be sent like a basket of lampreys on the back of a horseman to London or Windsor. The largest wagon the countryside could provide was needed for the removal of a sturgeon; such wagons were drawn by oxen and, even if the state of the roads permitted, an overland journey from Severn shore to London could not be made in less than a week. The Conqueror granted to the abbey of Gloucester all sturgeons taken in its waters. This privilege, which reverted to the Crown with the Reformation, is probably the first recorded instance of a 'Gloucestershire gift,' giving away something which one has no use for oneself. Similarly Henry II made a grant of all sturgeons and *pisces regales* taken in his manor to the Lord of Berkeley.

A man bringing a sturgeon to the castle in olden days was rewarded with a bow and arrow, and when bows and arrows were no longer in use the fisherman received a sovereign from the lord. Times are changed since the days when the lords of Berkeley fed a household of three hundred hungry men. To-day a sturgeon taken in Berkeley water may find its way to Billingsgate, not without some publicity, for this is news in the local and county press and may even make a couple of lines in Fleet Street. In normal times the fisherman receives from 5*d.* to 1*s.* 3*d.* a pound for his fish. But he has taken a sturgeon and that in his own and his fellow fishermen's estimation is honour above price.

E

It is characteristic of Purton that it should have run its own Derby, for in 1921 and 1922 pony races were run on Derby Day for a mile along Severn bank above Royal Drift. The field came from Cheltenham and elsewhere, but after two annual meetings the races were stopped, for it appeared that certain ponies had to win and 'some who seemed to be the best sports turned out to be the worst.' The Severn has since shown its disapproval of this event by eroding a great part of the course. But the river loves Purton and Purton men, and the land it has taken away from the race-course it has presented to the village in the form of a cricket ground, for in recent years a square level piece of ground well covered in grass has silted up in front of the 'Berkeley Arms.' It is a pleasant ground with the pub, a pavilion, and the river as boundaries. It is a six if you hit one over the four-foot wire netting that bounds the river, four if you hit the wire, and in the annals of Purton cricket there have only been three lost balls and those when the river was in full tide. It is a six if you hit the walnut-tree or the pub, and if you are lucky enough to break one of the windows of the 'Berkeley Arms' the landlord will not only bear the loss bravely, but will stand you a bottle of whisky as well. There have been many near misses, but the landlord has never had to pay up yet.

Within the shade of the walnut-tree four and a half steps lead down to the cricket field. They are all that are left showing of the twenty-two steps that led down to Purton Passage. In former times you could be ferried across here for a halfpenny. With the war Purton cricket fell into abeyance, yet the old men still sat under the tree as they watched young airmen at their bombing practice at a target out on Frampton Sand, and you heard the same remarks and even applause that you heard at a cricket match.

Purton is very proud of this walnut-tree and I cannot do

better than to tell its story, as it was told me by one who has known the tree all his life.

'That walnut-tree didn't make any growth at all for ten or fifteen years, and the stem remained about as thick as a man' leg with the head the size of one of those old-fashioned carriage umbrellas. That's thirty years ago or more; then a man said he'd kill or cure the tree. He was just a working man like myself and was half up the pole at the time with the cider he'd drunk. But you know how it is, you're twice as clever when you've had one over the eight. Well, he got the landlord's permission to have his way with the tree, kill or cure. He said the tree was rind-bound, and he took out his knife and slit the bark of the tree from top to bottom in eight or ten different slits. That's thirty years ago and the head of the tree's as big as it will ever get, though the bole's not done growing.'

The tree has, indeed, a fine head, though its scars have not yet healed, but have lengthened with its growth. At the time of this operation the slits were five feet six inches long and are now over eight feet. Before the bark was cut the bole was not more than fifteen inches round, now I can just put my two arms around the trunk.

Opposite Purton, across the river, is a hamlet of the same name though it has no parochial connection with the village. Sir Walter Raleigh stayed at Manor House Farm, the white house on the bluff overlooking the river, while his contemporary Sir Francis Drake sojourned in the next riverside hamlet of Gatcombe. These places lie on the edge of the Forest of Dean, where the forest land falls steeply to Severn shore, and Drake and Raleigh came here to buy timber for their ships. Gatcombe, now a sombre hamlet, was once the port for Blakeney and traded with Ireland, from where it imported food for the sustenance of the forest.

The field on top of the cliff enclosing Gatcombe was once a timber yard, and the ground at the foot of the cliff, now a dry dock for stopping-boats, is still called the barking-yard. Oak bark was stripped here and exported chiefly to Ireland.

When the railway was built through Gatcombe along Severn shore, Drake's house became an inn known as the 'Sloop,' but to-day there are not enough throats or visitors to Gatcombe to keep an inn going. One landlord of this inn was a victim of dropsy, and to cure him a hole was dug in his garden in which his swollen legs were buried. He remained in this position a whole week, a small shelter being built over his person to protect him from the weather. He obtained much relief from this primitive remedy though dropsy ultimately killed him. This strange treatment was carried out on the Gatcombe landlord between eighty and a hundred years ago.

The railway, embanking the river as it does for a mile above and two miles below Gatcombe, has robbed the hamlet of the riparian peace that it once possessed, and deprives the wayfarer of three pleasant miles of Severn shore. The Severn Bridge from Purton to Sharpness was opened in 1879 and is still admired locally. It is an impressive feat of engineering and surprised me the first time that I saw it, partly on account of its ugliness, for it is the only serious eyesore on the river and remains in view a long time. The builder constructed this bridge so that river traffic could pass beneath it. What would he say if he could return to see airmen in their Spitfires and Hurricanes diving beneath his bridge like swallows on the wing? I admired their daring, until I saw the men whose job it is to paint the bridge, hanging in their cradle, while an aircraft dashed past within a few feet of them.

Gatcombe is famous for its stopping-boats, and although several of these boats may be seen lying idle in the barking-yard, only one stopping-boat has been built at Gatcombe during the present century. The only man I know who has built a stopping-boat is Joe Wathan of Frampton, a boat builder by trade: he is also a skilled draughtsman with a taste for cartoons, a poet, and a stopping-boat fisherman.

A stopping-boat has something of the sturdiness of a lifeboat about her; she is twenty-two feet long and eight in the beam. When in use she and her companion stopping-boats are

moored to a steel rope, which runs from the shore to a considerable way out in the channel. In this position the stream is fished on the lave-net principle. Two large rimes as stout as oars cross the gunwale in the shape of a V to make a head-line of thirty-two feet, the net being fastened to the rimes. This weight of timber jutting so far overboard has to be balanced by a half hundredweight on each rime, and the weights are so adjusted in the boat that the rimes slant downwards into the water, leaving the head-line well submerged. In this position the rimes and mouth of the net face upstream, while the bosom, or purse of the net, is floating under the boat. Five strings are attached to the bosom, their other ends meeting on a three-foot forked stick, known as the tuning-fork, which stands upright in the centre of the boat. While fishing the fisherman has his right hand on the bunch of strings by the tuning-fork, and his hand by constant practice is highly sensitive to anything but tide running through his net. He feels a tug on a string and it is a signal to him that something has come into the net. It is most likely to be a salmon, though it may possibly be a twait in the spring or a flat-fish in the summer. He closes the net by lifting the rimes and head-line out of the water and this is done by applying his own weight to the ends of the rimes. The fish, unless he can break the net, has no means of escape. The fisherman gathers the bosom of the net and removes the fish by the cunning hole. This is a hole in the net, securely fastened by string, which is untied when the fish is to be landed.

Thousands of people every year get a glimpse of the stopping-boat fisherman at his work, for the great stopping-boat fishery on Severn lies where the Great Western Railway runs along the river bank towards South Wales. To those who see the fisherman standing upright in his sturdy boat moored in the river, this type of fishing may seem monotonous and even tame. There is, however, no more dangerous way of catching a salmon than with a stopping-boat, for the fisherman has to play himself against the force of the tide, and if the rimes are a weapon against the salmon they are also a weapon in the hands of the tide. The rimes often cause a heavy list when a sudden gush of tide takes control of the boat. This flood tide is especially dangerous, and Joe Wathan has often had to use all his strength and skill to prevent his boat from being overwhelmed, despite the steel rope. Once he was so near to disaster that, if one of these gushes had risen by as much as the black-lead mark of a pencil, he would have been overwhelmed.

At such times the fisherman usually casts rimes and net overboard. This is quite easily done in an emergency, as the fork of the two rimes is anchored to the well of the boat by the heel-rope. Every stopping-boat man has done this some time or another during his career and has had to recover his gear a mile or more up-river. If this rope is jammed he will have to jump for it, and jump as far away from his boat as possible so as not to be swept into the bosom of his own net and be drowned—a fate that every stopping-boat man dreads. In the past twenty years two out of eight stopping-boat men have been so drowned.

The fishery of Wellhouse Bay is worked by Joe Wathan and Harry Goulding, though in favourable times two others are fishing with them. Their fleet, like ships of the line, may be seen strung out in a little armada with but small space between the toes of their head-lines. Alternately they fish either the bottom or the top of the pool, according to the tide, and in carrying out their trade are following one of the ancient traditions of the River Severn. There is a comradeship between these men, and the age-long fraternity of stopping-boat fishermen is one of the traditions of the river.

In the little stone cabin under the railway embankment, the fraternity, temporarily reduced to two, has its home. The generation of stoppers, who have now passed on, proclaimed its unity in the following rhyme:

Jimmy from Ireland, Taffy from Wales,
If you believe me they could tell some good tales.
There was Turner the Ganger, Boshie a Snob,
And our young owner and old Red Knob.

Jimmy did not come from Ireland, but because Taffy was Henry Davies, who came from Wales, Jimmy was made to come from Ireland so that Taffy should feel more at home. Now it is just Joe and Harry in the Fish House, but while the chimney still smokes like an old man's pipe you know that as always there is more knowledge of Severn tide under that roof than anywhere else in the world.

Harry is the son of Boshie a Snob and wonders how his father received the nickname of Boshie. He had another nickname, that of Water Rat, which is carved in neat lettering on the fireplace in honour of one of his great physical feats. The rope mooring the boats needed replacing and fastening to a two-ton iron anchor in twelve feet of water. This was a task needing a diver, but Boshie went down and fixed the cable to the eye-bolt and came up three times 'for a blow' and thereby won for himself the dubious title of Water Rat. When over sixty years of age he was seen to jump a five-barred gate almost from a walk. The water below Severn Bridge was the scene of Boshie's one-man mutiny when he was mate of a trow. These vessels, which have now disappeared from the river, were two-masted sailing barges with plenty of sail. Below Severn Bridge the skipper wanted the topmast struck, but Boshie, who sensed the clearance of the bridge as well as he knew his own front doorway, said no.

'Thou hasn't.'

'Thee aren't.'

'Thou hasn't.'

'Thee aren't.'

So ran the argument between the skipper and his mate. Boshie said that he would rather risk his life than strike the topmast; to prove it he climbed to the top of the mast and stayed there while the trow sailed under the bridge, and as she did so Boshie triumphantly waved his arm above his head.

No fish no money is the rule of the stopping-boat fishermen and, though they work for a private owner, every fisherman is a very independent man. The owner of the fishery is the fisherman's boss 'up to a point,' but the owner pays the fisherman no retainer or wages and is consequently powerless to command his services. The owner pays all expenses, boat, nets, gear, repairs, and licences, in return for which he receives half the value of all salmon caught. The fisherman gets the other half. The returns on salmon fishing in Wellhouse Bay vary enormously. At present, even with a relative scarcity of fish, the high price of salmon makes fishing worth while and, after several lean seasons, the last day's catch I counted numbered a dozen fish. The stopping-boat fisherman deserves his days of plenty; Harry Goulding once fished for five weeks on end without earning fivepence, at another time his weekly share came to £50. The fishermen's half-share of the value of the fish taken is invariably shared equally between them, irrespective of individual luck. Any fish other than salmon which the fishermen catch are their exclusive property and any sewin caught belongs to them outright. To any other than a fisherman a sewin looks like another salmon, it eats like salmon and may be as big as twenty pounds. Three, four, or half a dozen of these fish are caught in a season and come as a pleasant surprise to the fisherman. A sewin differs from a salmon in the following ways: its tail is square, instead of being swallow-tailed as in the true fish, and when dead its body remains limp and does not go stiff as will a salmon's in *rigor mortis*. Harry Goulding has a theory that as a mule is to a horse so is the sewin to the true salmon; possibly one of the trout tribe plays the part of the paternal ass. Both he and Joe are convinced that the salmon eats nothing while in the river, but are of the opinion that the kilts when returning to the sea swim into the swarms of elvers and regain their strength on this nourishing diet. Joe's is the last true elver-net to be seen down-river, for his home is at Frampton and when he is down at Wellhouse Bay his net accompanies him. Joe Wathan's father was born in Minsterworth on Saint Valentine's Day. 'The midwife was busy, so grandfather picked up his elver-net and went down to the river to distract his mind. On dipping the net into the water he found the elvers swimming as thick as a horse's tail, and returned home with two

pailfuls to learn that his son had been born.' Elvers have
probably never been caught in the river so early in the year
as this before or since, the weather having been exceptionally
mild.

Elvering and catching a few sea fish are minor distractions
in the business of stopping-boat fishing. Some of the sea
fish caught are curious as the angler fish and the ink fish.
Of the ink fish, 'You could write a letter with it and the more
you let the tap run on it the more ink runs out,' says Joe,
who respects ink for he is a lover of fine literature. I shall
always remember his strong, gentle voice in the Fish House
below Severn Bridge reciting Francis Thompson's great poem
In no Strange Land. Though I knew this poem well, Joe knew
it by heart and he so understood its inner meaning that, by
reciting it, he made me understand things in the poem
which until then had eluded me. I have never heard a
poem read with greater beauty. Joe had no need of a book,
for the words live in his being. I left him that day wishing
that some of our fancy readers and actors, who hurriedly
recite poetry over the wireless to the multitude, could have
heard him. They would have become humbler and wiser.
The poetry of Francis Thompson gleams like the evergreen
mistletoe in Joe Wathan and there is an anthology of fine
poetry in Joe's 'log of memory.'

The stopping-boat fisherman breeds his own philosophy,
for when ruin seems to stare him in the face he never loses
heart. The motto of Wellhouse Bay Fish House is older than
much of our classical literature. It has lived for generations
in the minds and on the lips of fishermen and is here
committed to paper for the first time:

> Wherever the wind and whatever the tide
> There 's always good fishing by our fireside.

*E

XIII. BERKELEY

On account of its quicksands the Prinn is the most
dangerous fishing-ground in all the Severn. It lies just off
Sharpness, and one morning in the early light a fisherman
sank to his waist on these sands before he was rescued; the
experience so unnerved him that he never went into the river
again.

Below the ness the main channel of the river turns inshore,
and here the heathen Danes landed in the year 1000. They
made their home with one foot in their long boats and another
on the point of land they so appropriately named Sharpness,
which with the years has become one of the most explicit of
our place names.

The primitive tradition and almost primeval quiet on the
lower Severn is preserved through the maritime life of the
river being entirely focused on the port of Sharpness. The
port was made by the canal linking it with Gloucester. Nearer
than anywhere else to the industrial midlands, ocean-going
ships of up to 4,000 registered tons can dock at Sharpness,
while the canal takes vessels of up to 700 registered tons.
When the canal was completed in 1827, Sharpness was so
unknown that it became known as the Gloucester–Berkeley
Canal.

Sharpness is neither a town nor a village, it is a dock with
a confusion of roads and railway lines, short rows of red brick
houses, and innumerable swing and fixed bridges. Sharpness
men do not go to sea, but they make inland voyages to
Gloucester, Stourport, and other places in the midlands.
Scandinavians still come in their ships to Sharpness, but the
most colourful visitors from the north are the wild geese,
who arrive in their gaggles to spend the winter on the Severn.
They fill the gap between one salmon season and the next,
and give interest to the dull days of winter. They are the
most civilized of birds, and none are more regular in their

habits. I wonder what they feel when they return to New Grounds and find that their favourite patch of grass has been turned up by the plough.

I saw a large flock of these dispossessed wild geese feeding in the meadow in front of Berkeley Castle, not a hundred yards from the moat. In the bright January sun their chestnut plumage was only a shade darker than the rosy-grey of the castle walls. To see these most elusive birds, that haunt the loneliest pastures, within three minutes' walk from the centre of an English town was a matter of no small wonder. The nearby road was little frequented, and when I slipped through the stile between the palisade of trees, one or two birds fluttered uneasily, though the others, of whom there were between three and four hundred, continued feeding.

I have never had a better view of wild geese on the ground, where they stood so thick that I could see little pasture between their bodies, as they covered about a sixth of an acre. One step forward or the barest movement on my part would be enough to set them off in alarm. As it was, after watching them for five minutes, I coughed almost imperceptibly, but this, at a distance of a hundred yards, was enough to launch several hundred birds into an instantaneous gaggle of alarm. They lost some of their gregariousness in flight as the gaggle broke off into skeins, scattering in a mass confusion of thought, yet they gathered again from this untidiness, half in the air half on land, far enough to be beyond gunshot.

Some farmers do not like wild geese on their grounds and complain that they 'devour the young grass' at a time when there is none. However, they crop short grass of little value and generously manure the ground when it is most needed, and even in an hour their droppings will be well spread out over the land they have grazed.

Of all birds the life and habits of the wild goose most closely resembles the pattern of human existence. Like man this bird is a creature of habit and routine, and yet without variety he cannot live. In his daily life he combines the activities of eating and exercise, pleasure and good company. While most birds fritter their lives away in search of food, the wild geese have fixed and punctual hours for feeding and relaxation. In the middle of the morning they are to be seen in small social groups on the river. They spend the time flying, swimming, and resting, enjoying life and keeping fit.

At eleven o'clock the geese gather and fly to their chosen feeding-ground, and it is curious how the small groups will congregate into a large community for the midday meal. They eat from eleven till two, when they return to the river, and while the land is necessary for their sustenance the water is essential for their welfare, yet in spite of this highly gre-garious existence the wild goose leads a private and in-dividualistic life of absolute monogamy.

One winter's day, while walking along the sea wall from Sharpness to Berkeley, I disturbed a pink-footed goose from where he had lain under the river bank. He rose so slowly that for a split second I imagined that he was a heron, until I saw the vivid pink of his feet and the warm chestnut of his wings. He was wounded, and like all of his kind after being hit would spend his last hours or days of existence completely alone, at the end of a life in which he had never known solitude. Ignorant as we are of these creatures, we do not know whether the living forsake the dying or whether some inner spiritual force compels the doomed bird to await his end in loneliness. But whatever the reason, this line of behaviour is based on an instinct far surer than the shifting sands of human knowledge.

The goose flew out over the river and then turned towards the afternoon sun. His colour rapidly faded, but I could still see his movements above the slower tempo of the waves. I did not see him drop or descend to the water, but im-perceptibly his identity was merged in the fretful motion of the grey river. A lonely flight of migration, who knows whither?

Not far away, an old lave-net fisherman gathering driftwood for his winter's fire told me that a wounded goose will some-times live for three days, but that by then he will be useless for the pot, having wasted away to skin and bone.

This old man pronounced Berkeley as it is written, and not in the way that the town is more familiarly spoken of elsewhere. As we talked there was a shot from the direction of the town, and a few seconds later a gaggle of geese flew over our heads towards the river. Something in their arrangement told me that these were the same geese I had seen some minutes earlier, and without counting I knew that one of them was missing. Their voices, muffled by the gale, were disturbed and querulous, and before they reached the middle of the river the missing goose was attempting to join them.

The stricken bird was perhaps three hundred yards behind, but though he was able to keep up he was gradually losing altitude. Suddenly the scene became sordid and miserable. Except that the geese have no means of retaliation and defence, this was a horrible mimicry of aerial warfare, and for a moment the receding gaggle in their orderly formation become a flight of planes, the wounded bird something more than a machine.

These brief visitors add enormously to the beauty and interest of their surroundings at the least favoured time of the year. The wild goose is a bird of heart and guts, built for high flying over long distances, whose size is quite out of proportion to his value as a table-bird. He is spare, and a four-and-a-half-pound bird does not weigh very heavy when drawn and plucked for the pot. He deserves the hospitality of protection at present enjoyed by so many birds, and above all he should be protected from the poor marksman with an indifferent gun.

The sea wall turns abruptly inland at Berkeley Pill, where the Little Avon meanders beautifully into the main stream of the Severn. At high tide it has the grandeur of a river, but at low water it is the merest trickle, lost between steep mud banks. Although the town is only a mile away, the meanders of the Little Avon prolong this distance to at least three, and, before Sharpness became a dock, this pill was the port for Berkeley, the only one on this side of the river between Gloucester and Bristol.

It was still in use until about 1920, when Lord Fitzhardinge kept two sailing barges, the *Lavender* and the *Industry*, at

Berkeley. They could only be used at spring tides and brought cargoes of Chepstow stone for the repair of the roads, and coal from Lydney. In the past the pill brought considerable trade to Berkeley when '2*d*. wheelage was taken by the mayor for every wainload of coal, wine, oil, salt, and the like there unladen and carried through the town.'

Just below the town the Little Avon is joined by Matford Brook, and because it serves the mill and has been artificially widened to improve the view from the castle, the brook is often mistaken for the river. Where it turns the corner of the park by the kennels of the Berkeley Hunt the brook falls in a weir up which, until the beginning of the century, salmon were seen to leap. This was no idle frolic, for the fish spawned in the brook, which is, I believe the only water where salmon have spawned in any tributary or sub-tributary of the tidal Severn. Though if they have spawned here it is surprising that they have not ventured up the Swilgate or the Leadon, though the Frome has been impregnated for centuries by the mills of Stroud, and the streams from Dean have been contaminated for even longer by mine workings. Salmon no longer leap the cascade of Matford water since the weir was heightened by the Fishery Board to prevent their doing so.

It is hard to see what useful purpose was served, indeed it would seem that the very reverse was achieved, by this interference with the natural instinct of the fish. Possibly authority took the view that a salmon in this brook was too easy a prey in a district where almost any man is a potential poacher of the fish. But if salmon were still to spawn in the water of Matford Brook there would probably be more fish in the river. Too many fish are defeated or killed by the polluted water of the midlands before they reach the spawning-beds in Wales, and pinks spawned in Matford Brook should have a better chance of survival than those which have to make the long and dangerous river journey to the sea.

In the days when salmon spawned in Matford Brook the Severn was crowded with fish and many mated salmon were glad to turn aside into this water. Any instinct they may have had to do so has probably been lost, yet if salmon could be encouraged to reach this water and there enjoy reasonable protection, it would result in there being more fish in the river in years to come.

The castle, as seen from the brook, is a well-dressed building that reflects the elegance of Plantagenet England. Shakespeare is thought to have been familiar with a distant prospect of Berkeley Castle, for in *King Richard II*, when lost in 'the wilds in Glostershire,' he makes Percy exclaim:

'There stands the castle, by yon tuft of trees.'

Act III, scene iii.

From which we may even find the point where he, Bolingbroke, and Northumberland were standing, which must have been on the brow of Stinchcombe Hill.

Edward II was murdered in the castle with such brutality that, according to a local tradition, his screams were heard three miles away. Though denuded of its fortifications, the building has the splendour of a palace of the Middle Ages, and its setting is enhanced by standing in a district poor in domestic architecture.

Berkeley with its three main streets, one of them a dead end, is little more than a village, though a compactness in its undetached houses and its ancient prestige give it the dignity of a town. There is a an undisturbed eighteenth-century air about the place, which fills the visitor with nostalgia for the past.

Many kinds of fish have been caught off Berkeley, and more than three hundred years ago fifty-three different specimens were recorded by John Smyth of Nibley. Though his list would not satisfy a marine biologist, or even a fisherman of to-day, it is at least entertaining in its variety.

'Sturgeon, porpoise, Thornpole, Jubertas or young whale, herringe, hogge, seal, swordfish, salmon, wheat trout or fuen, Turbot, Lamprey, Lampern, Shad Tweat, wray, the houndfish, the dogfish, the sole, the flooke, the flounder, the sand flooke (resembling the sole), a barne, a cod, a card, an eel pout, a mackarell, the sunfish, the hake, an haddock, a Roncote, the sea tad, a plaice, the millet, also mullet, Ling, dabbe, yearling, horncake, the Lumfish, A gurnard both red and grey, a cuttlefish, a whiting, a little crab, the Conger also the Conger eel being the hee fish, the she fish is called a quaver, the dorrey, the huswife, the herring, the sprat, the pilchard, the prawn, the shrimp, the eel, a fauzon or great fat eel. Elvers supposed by some to be the young eel, the base, the sea bream and the Halibut.'

Smyth was a steward to the Berkeleys and a lover of good food, for he remarks that 'in this part of the river the prime season for the goodness of salmon goes out when the buck comes in and comes in when the buck goes out.' He calls the sole 'our Seaverne Capon . . . a meat of prime note,' and adds that 'the belly of a sturgeon is preferred before the back, and the lesser the sturgeon the more wholesome and tender is its flesh.'

There were plenty of buck then at Berkeley, for Queen Elizabeth I, much to the annoyance of the lord, killed twenty-seven stags in a day's hunting, and added insult to injury by remarking that the lord did not give sufficient attention to his oaks.

The lamprey was not a royal fish on which the lord made a traditional payment. Sturgeon, seal, thornpole, and porpoise were *pisces regales*, but, says Smyth with a word of warning to the zealous, 'the lord makes no retribution for whales.' In his emphatic style, without adding a word, he implies the disappointment and ill feeling at Berkeley on the following recorded occasion.

'A 22 ft. young whale or Jubertas was caught in 1620 (a picture was drawn of it in the Great Hall at Berkeley Castle) and no retribution was made for the making of the great dray on which the fish was drawn where at were tyed 35 yoke of oxen. The fish yeilded an oil then said and still believed to be very soveraigne and medicinable for aches, etc.'

The fisheries of the manor of Berkeley belonged to the lord, but fishermen also had their rights and this sometimes accounted for the very high price which even the king had to pay for his fish. A little above Berkeley 'the tide floweth

THE HORSESHOE BEND OF SEVERN TIDE:
THE VIEW FROM POPE'S HILL

three hours and ebbeth nine hours twice in each twenty-four,'
and of these tides one tide every week was known as the lord's
tide: 'When the lord hath all the fishes in certain places taken
thereat, and the next tide is called the Parson's tide, for his
tithe fish. The lord's on Thursday, the parson's on the
Friday the next after.' And fishermen being what they are
no doubt fished with less enthusiasm on these days and allowed
a salmon to slip past their nets. At certain places and seasons
of the tide any stranger might fish with a lave-net (but not
with a long-net or draught-net) and take any fish except
pisces regales, shad, gilling salmon (the full-grown fish), and
lampreys.

The fish he was allowed to catch were known as galeable
fish. This meant that the lord of the manor had a half
interest in all fish so taken. The lord, or his lessee or agent,
who was known as the galor, might choose whether he would
take the fish and pay half the price to the fisherman, or refuse
the fish and demand that the fisherman pay half the price.
A fisherman might legally escape gale by running with the
fish as far as beyond the high-tide mark before the galor
could come, cry, or call to him. He then stuffed grass into
the fish's mouth as token that his catch was free of gale.
Even if there were many galors, they could not patrol all the
eighteen miles of the shore of the manor of Berkeley, but gale
fishing was only allowed at low water, so that fishermen
usually had a long way to run before touching down on grass.

The system of gale probably made for a fair price, but in
the course of time a dispute arose between fishermen and the
lord's galor, as to who should set the price of galeable fish.
It ended in a troublesome suit in the Court of Chancery in
1607, which ruled that the fisherman should set the price of
his fish.

By an ancient custom all fish caught in the manor were
brought to the market cross in Berkeley, where they had to
remain for an hour before the fisherman was allowed to carry
and sell the fish outside the hundred. In the absence of the
lord and his chief officers, fishermen, who no doubt got a

better price further afield, began to evade this custom, until a dowager Lady Berkeley insisted on its revival.

Gale resulted in the lords of Berkeley, and even the king, having to pay very high prices for lampreys. The Berkeleys like all families who remain rich kept careful accounts and records, even in illiterate times. These show that in Berkeley a lamprey could cost more than £1 apiece and Maurice, Lord Berkeley, had to pay £6 7s. 2d. for six lampreys he sent as a present to Edward III. In no reign can the Berkeley family position have been more precarious, for though the Lord of Berkeley proved by dubious alibi that he was away from his castle at the time of Edward II's murder, the family can never have gained favour with his son.

Henry I's death from a surfeit of lampreys did not curb the appetite of his successors for the fish. King John was a great glutton for lampreys, and his son Henry III inherited his royal greed; possibly no king or commoner, before or since, has eaten so many of this fish. No year of his long reign passed without this king having his lampreys from the Severn, and from as far away as Canterbury the king ordered the sheriff 'to bake for him all the lampreys he can get and send them him by his cook. And that when he shall be nearer Severn, then to send them unbaked so long as they may come sweet, for him and his queen to eat.'

One February this king ordered the sheriff to forbid any man to buy lampreys, 'but that he buy and send them to the king wheresoever he be for all Lent.' History shows that even kings object to paying high prices for their meals, and Henry even instituted price control for the benefit of his own pocket by forbidding any man to sell a lamprey for more than two shillings. There is a comical touch worthy of nursery rhyme in Henry's command to the sheriff to send him two parts of all the lampreys he can buy or get to Norwich, and the other third part to the queen at Windsor Castle.

In Berkeley an event took place that has affected the entire world, for here Jenner discovered vaccination, and by one of those perverse paradoxes of humanity, Gloucester has remained

a stronghold of the anti-vaccinationists, which more than once
has resulted in violent local outbreaks of smallpox. I even
know of an anti-vaccinationist who has lived all her life
within three miles of Berkeley.

One morning on Over Bridge I found myself earmarked
for propaganda by one of Gloucester's anti-vaccinationists.
He maintained his attitude with the fervour of a fanatic towards
a taboo, and the general drift of his inspired nonsense came
across like a speech by one of the more foolish characters in a
Ben Jonson play.

Berkeley was not only the birthplace of Edward Jenner, it
was his home and the natural laboratory of his genius. He
was born in the old vicarage in 1749, and Berkeley might have
seen little of him, for his father died when he was a small
boy, had not his elder brother succeeded as vicar. He was
educated in Gloucestershire, where he showed an exceptional
flair for scientific knowledge by collecting fossils and the nests
of dormice. An unusual hobby for a boy in the middle of the
eighteenth century, when an interest in natural history was
only rarely to be met with among the elderly erudite. On
leaving school he was apprenticed to Ludlow, the surgeon at
Chipping Sodbury, and it was here that he overheard the
famous remark made by a young woman, who said: 'I cannot
take smallpox, for I have had the cowpox.'

At twenty-one Jenner left Gloucestershire to study at St.
George's Hospital under its famous surgeon John Hunter.
In Jenner Hunter found a congenial pupil, for Hunter besides
being a doctor was an omnivorous naturalist, owning a
menagerie at Brompton and collecting any rare or unusual
specimen of natural history. When Captain Cook returned
from his first voyage of Australian discovery, Jenner, through
Hunter's influence, had the job of arranging the botanical
and natural history specimens Cook had brought home with
him. This task was so carefully and skilfully carried out by
Jenner that he was offered the post of naturalist on Cook's
next voyage of discovery. It is tantalizing to conjecture upon
the possibilities which then lay within Jenner's grasp. When

Jenner was sixty a boy was born in a house overlooking the River Severn at Shrewsbury: his name was Charles Darwin, who as a young man sailed round the world in H.M.S. *Beagle* and afterwards wrote the book that reorientated modern thought. From Jenner's note-books, the jottings of later years, the following extract finds him groping at the theory of evolution.

'The student of geology scarcely passes the threshold of his inquiry before he finds himself in a bewildered country. The Mosaic account of the deluge on one side, and the order in which he finds the mineral cabinets arranged by the hand of nature on the other.'

But Jenner declined the offer of sailing as naturalist to Captain Cook's expedition; he also refused Hunter's offer of a partnership. It is well for the world that he did so. He turned from the prospects of fame and eminence to the obscurity of practising medicine in his native Berkeley. His association and friendship with Hunter continued happily. Hunter was continually writing to his old pupil for specimens, and Jenner must have had many talks with salmon fishermen in his attempts to satisfy Hunter's demands for a large porpoise 'for love or money,' salmon spawn, eels, and cuckoos. They jointly made investigations into the hibernations of hedgehogs, and Hunter from London wrote to Jenner asking for 'a true and particular account of the cuckoo and as far as possible under your own eye.' A full job for a trained ornithologist, and the busy country doctor set his young nephew Harry to watch a nest with a cuckoo's egg while he was away on his rounds. From Harry's and his own observations Jenner prepared a paper, which Hunter submitted to the Royal Society in 1787. This was the first authentic account of how the young cuckoo ejects the eggs of its foster parents from the nest. The president of the society, however, acknowledged Jenner's contribution with polite but definite doubt: 'In consequence of your having discovered that the young cuckoo, and not the parent bird, removes the egg from the nest in which it is deposited, the council thought it best to give you

full scope for altering it as you shall choose. Another year
we shall be glad to receive it again, and print it.'

Jenner deserves an even more honoured place in the history
of British ornithology for having surmised, without definite
proof, the mystery of bird migration, in an age when England's
most famous naturalist, Gilbert White, destroyed a roof of
thatch in winter in search of a hibernating swallow.

Jenner's practice covered a large and unhealthy area of the
English countryside, for in his day ague, which has long since
completely disappeared, was still common in the Vale of
Berkeley and, though there was little the doctor could do for
this ill, it increased the complications in his patients' other
maladies. His days were largely spent in the saddle, for his
rounds often covered a circuit of twenty to thirty miles, and
in his broad-brimmed hat, blue coat, brass buttons, and high
well-polished boots, he looked the typical country gentleman
of his day. These rides were seldom lonely, for the miles would
often be lightened by the company of a neighbour or two,
who would ride with him for the pleasure of his conversation.
His relations with his patients were all that a good doctor's
should be, for, says Baron his biographer, 'his knowledge and
dexterity as a surgeon, his manners as a gentleman, and his
general information rendered his company always acceptable.
. . . He not only commanded confidence by his skill, but also
secured to himself goodwill and affection by his tenderness,
kindness and benevolence of his nature.'

Doctors are chary of interests beyond their profession, but
Jenner in addition to his scientific interests, outside the scope
of medicine, was also a poet and a musician. He played the
violin in the local musical club and wrote a number of poems.
His verses are of real literary merit and reflect the acute
observation of his mind. His best poems are on Berkeley
Fair, not an easy theme, and on a Robin. These distractions
did not prevent the doctor from joining a society of medical
men, who met at Alveston where they read papers and held
discussions, and he was the chief founder of a similar society
that met in the Fleece Inn at Rodborough. One may picture

these eighteenth-century medicos sitting down to a good dinner before a roaring fire. One can catch the muffled murmur of the speaker's voice behind closed doors as he addressed the meeting that preceded it. Jenner read papers at these meetings on angina pectoris, ophthalmia, valvular disease of the heart, and cowpox.

In his middle forties Jenner nearly died from an attack of typhus. Convalescence provided his mind with leisure, during which he came to conclusions regarding cowpox and smallpox that he soon put to the test. Sarah Nelmes, a milkmaid, had a hand infected with cowpox, and from it Jenner extracted vesicles and with this he vaccinated James Phipps, an eight-year-old boy, in two places. This simple operation, the first of countless millions, was performed in the square summer-house with its roof of heavy thatch, that still stands under the churchyard wall in the corner of Jenner's garden, on 14th May 1796, three days before Jenner's forty-seventh birthday. Six weeks later the doctor inoculated the boy with smallpox with negative results. To some this procedure might seem unethical, but inoculation against smallpox had been introduced from the East by Lady Mary Wortley Montagu, and consisted in exposing the patient when in health to a milder form of the disease. Jenner had as a child been immunized against smallpox by this dangerous means and had suffered terribly through being confined in a stable during this process. Few men, possibly only Sir Ronald Ross, who wrote a poem commemorating his discovery of the cause of malaria, have shared the sensations that were Jenner's in the hour of his achievement. 'The joy I felt,' he wrote, 'at the prospect before me of being the instrument destined to take away from the world one of its greatest calamities . . . was so excessive that I sometimes found myself in a kind of reverie.'

If Jenner had practised elsewhere than in the Vale of Berkeley, where dairying is the chief industry, the chances of his making this discovery would indeed have been remote. It is an exception for a brilliant doctor to practise in the depths of the country, and vaccination might have gone undiscovered for another century; as it was, a temporary disappearance of cowpox held up further experiments. The greatness of Jenner's discovery lies in the fact that he should have discovered without hesitancy the method of vaccination, which has remained unaltered for a century and a half. He has enabled all subsequent medical thought to take a new view of the conquest of disease. He is the common ancestor of preventive medicine.

Jenner went to London with no thought of financial gain from his great discovery, which he gave to the world. After a few initial difficulties, scepticism and professional jealousies, not only England but Europe accepted vaccination, and in his lifetime the practice of vaccination spread to the North American Indians, India, and even China. Jenner in his own words became 'the vaccine clerk of the world.' He left Berkeley and with it the income from his practice, so Parliament by a mean majority of three voted him a grant of £10,000. For a while he practised in Mayfair, but had little love for the city and its ways, and left London for Cheltenham. It was one step back on the road to Berkeley. Gifts that would flatter the heart of an emperor were bestowed upon him. He was honoured by universities at home and abroad. But Jenner, who was one of the world's truly great men, accepted them at their worth. Characteristically the Royal Society of Physicians refused a fellowship to the greatest name in medicine, unless Jenner, like a university undergraduate, passed the usual examinations in Latin, and, with characteristic good humour, Jenner said that he would not fulfil this condition 'even for the whole of John Hunter's museum.'

'Cheltenham,' wrote Jenner, in a letter to a friend, 'is too gay for me. I still like my rustic haunt old Berkeley best.' And after the death of his wife he returned home. Berkeley was unchanged and so, too, for all his world-wide fame was the doctor. James Phipps, whom he had vaccinated at the age of eight, was now suffering from tuberculosis and Jenner built him a cottage and helped with his own hands to plant his garden.

He became a magistrate, the only one in the town, and listened to the plaints and peccadilloes of salmon fishermen. He knew the parts of the lave-net as well as he knew the bones of the hand, and the Severn sand-banks and channels like the organs of the human body. To the end he followed the flights of birds, and his paper on bird migration was read to the Royal Society soon after his death in 1823. He had a stroke two years before his death, but was active unto the end. His last act was to walk to Ham on a cold afternoon in January to arrange for the distribution of fuel to the poor. To the cottagers he appeared not as the world-famous name, who had earned the gratitude of millions, but as their familiar friend. As he walked home alone, an aged figure whom life had left solitary, he looked for the last time on the place he loved so well, the red brick town on the hill with its stone-built tower and its castle behind the trees. I like to think that a gaggle of wild geese gladdened this last half hour, and that his thoughts at the last brooded on the migration of birds.

He was found next morning unconscious on the floor of his library, his right side was paralysed and he died on the following day. He shares with Shakespeare the honour of lying in the chancel of the parish church of his native town, not a hundred yards from the spot where he made his great discovery. He has and needs no memorial beyond the tablet of marble that records his name, and it would please him well that in a changing world Berkeley remains as he left it.

XIV. THE SEA WALL

Except for a few salmon fishermen no one in or about Berkeley takes any pleasure in the Severn, yet this was not always so, for six hundred years ago Thomas, Lord Berkeley, kept 'his barge for his delight and recreations, as well upon the haven as the river of Severn, in which were his sea furnitures in sumptuous manner.'

The road leading to the river ends at a farm, and beyond it no well defined path leads to the sea wall. A lonely little pepper-box of a house, long shuttered, standing among the pine-trees, overlooks the river; too small for a home for any but a hermit, it served as a look-out and a hunting lodge for the lords of Berkeley on their wild-fowling expeditions. Here at high tide you may stand and watch the ships go by on their way from Sharpness. They are small ships and may belong to any of the seafaring nations of Europe. There are coasters, and tugs with strings of barges. A little pageant of shipping passes within a stone's throw of the sea wall, and to complete the picture the rear is brought up by a sloop. Her mainsail is unfurled, but she has hardly come to terms with the wind, she has the air of a slattern who completes her toilet as she hurries down the street. But she quickly regains her composure, and with it the dignity of one who has survived her generation. In all her trim she has the grace of a dream ship, but the illusion is quickly lost as the mate pegs his trousers to the rigging, where they belly like a wind-sock in the breeze. The sloop is a long way behind the convoy, but she follows the wake of the pilots.

On their voyages up-river, pilots sometimes have problems other than those of navigation. I drank a pint of beer with one of them in Portishead while he was waiting for his ship. He had just been piloting a Rumanian vessel, whose captain was overcome with emotion on arriving at Shakespeare's native land for the first time. The Rumanian talked so much about Shakespeare that before they had gone a knot the pilot was out of his depth. The conversation soon became a one-sided affair as the captain bombarded the pilot with gossip and quotations from our national poet. All that the pilot knew about Shakespeare could be told in two minutes, but his skill and nerve withstood a recitation from the shipwreck scene in *The Tempest*, spoken in outlandish Balkan accents.

'As soon as he got ashore,' said the pilot, 'away he went to Stratford, and on our way down-river back to sea he didn't talk quite so much.' I wonder what had happened to the Rumanian; had he been disillusioned by Shakespeare's Stratford, or had he found the English a less genial and passionate people than Shakespeare had led him to believe? Anyway we must rejoice with him and envy him his literary pilgrimage, that he sailed his ship up the river fed by Shakespeare's Avon.

'And,' ended the pilot, in his slow nautical voice, 'I called him Svengali because he had a long black beard.'

Of all the world's writers who have achieved international reputation only Shakespeare has attained universal renown. Dante and Goethe are known to the schoolmen of lands other than their own, but Shakespeare has won for himself the admiration of the ordinary man beyond the land of his birth, and in this he stands unique among all writers, ancient or modern.

Pilots have a proper sense of their own importance, and to have Shakespeare thrown in his teeth by a bearded foreigner from the Black Sea in some obscure way wounded the pilot's pride.

The river quickly empties of its shipping, and a narrow damp ribbon on the stone face of the slope of the sea wall shows that the tide is on the ebb. In a matter of minutes the inch has lengthened to a foot. There are few greater contrasts in land and water than that which lies on either side of this sea wall; on one hand lies the sea, on the other a landscape typical of the midlands, green pastures, rambling hedgerows, and tall elm-trees. This land was once the Forest of Horwood, which extended from here as far as Bristol until it was fellep about the time when Hardinge, Reeve of Bristol, became Lord of Berkeley. Until Jenner's day the vale presented the appearance of rough parklands and remained unenclosed almost up to the time that he made his great discovery. The farming in the vale was then in a very primitive and un-improved condition, largely due to the great fertility of the soil, and this land is still in the fortunate position of being able to weather any agricultural crisis, for it is equally well suited for growing corn or fattening stock.

The sea wall is a great ramp of earth, grey on the river side where it is faced with stone, and green with grass to the landward. Though the wall dates from the Middle Ages it is only kept intact through constant repair, and the high tides backed by south-westerly gales in the autumn of 1945 breached the wall in three places along this reach of river. As a result of this success by the forces of nature, the wall is at present being reinforced by another three yards of Severn mud plastered on its inner side.

You may walk all day along the sea wall, but it demands your solitude for it hardly allows for two walking abreast. On one side are the birds of the sea, on the other those of the field and, except for such well-defined exceptions as the goose, the gull, the heron, and the crow, there are few birds that cross the sea wall into unfamiliar territory. At high water the cormorant patrols the lonely waves, flying only a few feet above the surface, sometimes with a flat-fish or an eel half twisted round his beak. At a distance the cormorant is often mistaken for a crow, for this bird is a great frequenter of the river and, as the gull shares his fields, so he feasts on the carrion of the shore, and not always carrion for, like the gull, the crow has been known to attack the living salmon. When an unfortunate fish has become landlocked and powerless in a shallow pool from which the tide has receded, these brutal birds, whether they be white or black, will immediately pluck out its eye.

Among the pleasanter birds, though by no means invariably present, is the beautiful sheldrake, or barrow duck as he is called locally, with his white-and-black plumage. On a summer's day I watched one of these birds floating with her young within a few feet of the sea wall, while at an equal distance on the other side of the wall a maternal plover was hustling her brood with alarm at my approach. But the most frequent and never absent bird is the sea snipe or spurre, the names by which the dunlin is usually known hereabouts.

One cannot walk very far along the sea wall or shore without disturbing a wisp of these birds, whom with their protective colouring one would otherwise have passed unnoticed. They fly outwards and then curve back inwards towards the sea wall, their flight is rapid and their call incessant, yet for all their vitality there is a peculiar melancholy about sea snipe, for their call is plaintive and cheerless, their colouring toneless.

A little below Berkeley Pill the Severn curves away from the sea wall, and the rapid ebbing of the tide uncovers a large waste of mud and rocks known as Hills Flats. This, as well as the other rocky seaweed-strewn wastes, is farmed no less thoroughly than the pasture or arable within the sea wall. At all times of the year the tide uncovers the great basket fisheries which are fixed to the floor of the river in weirs. In river parlance these ancient devices for catching fish are known as fixed engines, and are made up of kipes, butts, and foreweels.

In the days of early spring, here and there along the river bank, one may meet a solitary fisherman weaving a kipe. He takes a score of seven-foot hazel staves, which he pushes into the turf at a slant in a circle fifteen inches across. This is the most ancient of crafts still to be practised in Britain. It is prehistoric in origin and may even have had its beginnings in neolithic times. Its practice is entirely confined to the lower Severn and its open estuary, where it undoubtedly originated.

The first eighteen inches of the kipe are the most difficult to weave, and are also the most important, since on their structure depends the finished shape of the basket. It takes an experienced man half a day to make a kipe, and when he pulls this gigantic basket from the ground he will need all his

A NEWLY WOVEN KIPE BESIDE THE BERKELEY SEA WALL

strength to carry it. The completed kipe looks like a crinoline made for a giantess; from the slender waist the skirts swell to a diameter of eight feet at the hem.

The kipe is only the mouth to the fisherman's elaborate trap and is fixed so that it faces up-river. To the narrow waist of the kipe there is fitted another basket of closely woven withy, the butt, which to continue the simile may be compared with the bodice of the crinoline. The butt, like the kipe, has an open end to which is fitted another smaller basket, the foreweel, the end of this being stopped with either turf or seaweed.

Some basket fisheries run from the sea wall, but many lie far out in the bed of the river, and the number of kipes to each weir is fixed by law based on ancient precedent. Many of these basket fisheries belong to farms and some of them are leased by farmers to fishermen. Several are no longer in use, for when a farmer who has not been bred to kipe-making takes a riverside farm he sometimes lets the fishery lapse.

Stakes, often cemented into the rocks, are planted to hold the kipes and to these each kipe is fastened by a rod and pin. The rod is a thong of withy, expertly twisted, for in the hands of a basket fisherman a two-year-old shoot of withy can be turned into a stiff rope in a few seconds. The growing end of the withy is held under the foot while the fisherman spins the wand with a rapid movement of his hands; the withy, thus pliant, is twisted back on itself and plaited like rope in tight spirals to a rod, leaving a noose smaller than a penny at the end. The rod is bound through the kipe on to the stake but no tie is made. The pin, a stout six-inch peg of hazel, is pushed through the noose of the rod; a sharp twist, like a tourniquet, is then made and the pin driven home.

No knot of any kind is made and the rod-and-pin binding has the effect of weaving the kipe to the stake; this hold is stronger than the stoutest nail or rope. A similar fixture, known as the tail key, holds the butt to the kipe. The butt is about four feet long, slightly tapering where it joins the kipe, elongating into a tunnel large enough to take the biggest salmon. This basket is supported from the river bed on sticks and its end is open to receive the mouth of the fore-weel. The foreweel, usually pronounced 'voreel,' is sometimes known as the bottle, which it resembles in shape, and is about two feet six inches long with a chale, known as the churr, half way up its middle. The foreweel is supported on a forked stick on to which it is held down by the apse, a manacle of withy with a noose at either end that slips over the prongs of the stick. An apse looks an intricate piece of basket-work, but I have watched a fisherman weave one from a wand of red withy in twenty seconds.

The kipes are thus set up with butts and foreweels attached in a weir of anything from ten to eighty-three kipes. The potential of the kipes is in many cases greatly increased when the weir is continued in a blind line on either side, known as hedging and lining. This consists of stakes in the river bed through which rough basket-work is woven, rather like a hedge that has been newly laid. A fish coming against the hedging will swim along it, and the chances are that it will turn into the mouth of a kipe. Once in the kipe it may momentarily nose against its wicker sides, but it cannot swim backwards and instinct and the tide force it into the butt.

This type of fish-trap, surely the most ingenious ever devised by man, will catch anything from a sturgeon to a shrimp. A salmon will usually be lodged in the butt, with its head sticking into the foreweel, but behind the churr of the foreweel shrimps, eels, and whiting will be found at the ebb of the tide. At low tide the fisherman walks out to his weir with a witcher on his back; this is a curious basket, slightly broader than his shoulders, nine inches across, and two feet deep. Into the witcher he empties the foreweels, and places in it the salmon that he pulls from the butts.

So many sea fish used to be caught in these weirs, that up to about fifty years ago three or four men used to come to the river every day with their carts to collect the fish, which they hawked through Berkeley, Thornbury, Chipping Sodbury, and other towns and villages. By an extraordinary change in taste and custom the only fish that was almost unsaleable was the lamprey.

Though these fisheries are private, sturgeon taken off the manor of Berkeley still belong to the lord of the manor, but I have heard of fishermen who have taken sturgeon and left them to rot on account of the expense of taking them ashore. There is little inducement to carry a fish, perhaps weighing a hundredweight, over a mile of rock and seaweed and then transport it eight or ten miles to the castle to receive a bounty of £1 for doing so.

On the other hand, a young fisherman has told me that his father once brought a nineteen-pound sturgeon to the castle, on which, because of its relative smallness, they were unwilling to pay the £1 ordained by custom. Sturgeon can be extremely small. Some years ago in the bazaar of the Albanian town of Scutari, I bought a sturgeon, caught fresh from the lake, which is joined by a river to the nearby Adriatic, for something less than half a crown. It was not more than twenty inches long, but it made an excellent dinner for myself and two friends, with enough left over to gladden the cook, whose name was Socrates.

I had another meal of sturgeon in the lean days of the war when an entire fish was being displayed on a fishmonger's slab in Cheltenham. It was being retailed at six shillings a pound and had it been salmon people would have clamoured for it, but after it had been on show for a whole day I was the only person to buy a pound, and though I have eaten the famous koran salmon trout of Lake Ohrid, I have never tasted better fish than this; its flavour, though rarer, was not unlike that of the breast of turkey. This sturgeon was not caught in the Severn, but had, I believe, been taken in the sea off Milford Haven.

Though a public fisherman is not allowed to fish within fifty yards of a basket weir, most kipe fishermen are adept with the lave-net, and it is a great advantage to have a weir of kipes where the tide leaves a pool in the foreground when it may be fished with a lave-net. The best weirs are those through which the tide flows longest, and a good weir takes more fish than a long-net, a stopping-boat, or lave-net. It is, however, proportionally costly in labour and material. A highly skilled man will make two kipes in a day, they will last two or at best three seasons in the water, and a man will have to work very hard and very skilfully to make a kipe, a butt, and a foreweel in a day.

I know a farmer who owns two fisheries, one with forty-two, the other with ten kipes; these are flanked by eighty-three and a hundred and seventy-six yards of hedging, which have to be renewed every four years. He is the only man on his farm capable of this highly skilled work, and it takes up from three to four months of his working year.

A kipe is so cumbersome and heavy that it is usually dragged out to its mooring on a sled. When fixed to the weir it remains there until lost, destroyed, or worn out, but at the end of the salmon season in August the butts and foreweels are removed, allowing fish to pass through the kipe without danger. A butt made of withy is as finely woven as a shopping basket, but the kipe is of stronger, coarser weave. Its struts are stout as a man's thumb, its wicker the thickness of a lady's little finger, but even so the strongest kipe is soon worn out by the constant friction of the tide.

Every year kipes are lost, and a storm on a rising or ebbing tide may even carry an entire weir away. Often a weir is half wrecked by floating timber, and the keels of passing ships, who on a very high tide neglect to keep to the channel of the river, sometimes destroy a number of kipes. The most serious damage within living memory to the kipe weirs occurred in the winter of 1940 when the upper river was frozen over and the ice was broken by the Bore. Great slabs of ice, some of them weighing half a ton, came pounding against the kipe weirs, breaking them from their anchorage, and in the following summer only a small proportion of them were able to be replaced. In the latter days of January the fisherman goes down to review his losses and assess how much hazel he will have to buy, for the nut does not grow near here, though the withy is plentiful.

When one considers the labour involved, it is hard on the kipe fisherman that his season is limited from April to August: a lifetime ago they fished from February to September, and before that all through the year with consequent casualties among kilts returning to the sea. Out-of-season fishing is now confined to a little shrimping and the capture of eels. These are taken in an eel well, a weel baited with shrimps. The conger eel, too, is taken when left by the tide, particularly in the autumn and spring, when according to a local saying 'the moon and frost will kill the conger.'

Dutch grass is the worst weed this part of the Severn has ever known. It was introduced by Jenner Fust, the squire of Hill, who imagined that he would reclaim muddy wastes of the Severn into useful pasture. It reclaimed very little ground for him and did untold harm to others, for the grass made little headway against his property, but spread up and down and even across the river. This grass takes a firm deep root in mud and will thrive though submerged twice a day under salt water. Where it takes root against a basket fishery no fish will come, since they avoid swimming over grass. I have seen a putcheon fishery across the river ruined for a season's fishing by the encroachment of this grass. The squire meant well, but as someone once said to me, 'he ought to be made to come back and dig every bit of it out.'

He had, however, his friends among the lave-net men, for though he possessed several basket fisheries, he never objected to the lave-nets fishing in the vicinity of his fixed engines. In the past farmers found that their basket fisheries were a cheap means of feeding their labourers. Well into the last century the price of Double Gloucester cheese was fixed for the coming season every October at Barton Fair, Gloucester. At this festival of the farming year, farm servants hired themselves out to new masters for the next twelve months, and when approached by a riverside farmer they would stipulate that they should not be fed on salmon.

F

All that remains of Horwood Forest is a small wood lying under the sea wall, which has, one suspects, been preserved as a foxes' covert for the Berkeley Hunt. Sometimes a hunted fox who knows the river well will run out over Hills Flats where he may succeed in throwing hounds off his scent, but as there is scarcely any cover, except behind a kipe weir, hounds continue to hunt him by sight. This is, however, a clever move on the part of the fox, for the huntsman cannot bring his horse down the slippery face of the sea wall, and by the time the fox has regained the grasslands hounds may well be checked before they pick up scent again. Vale foxes are cunning; recently a hunted fox gave hounds a run to Aust Cliff where he had the satisfaction of seeing ten hounds plunge over the precipice to their death.

Close to Hill Pill the holy thorn blooms at Christmas. Local tradition, which does not spread much further than the village of Hill, maintains that Joseph of Arimathaea preached here and that the thorn grew from the staff he stuck in the ground. If Joseph came to Britain and if he went to Glastonbury, what should be more likely than that he should come to Hill, which for all its past and present remoteness is a simple voyage from Avalon up the Somerset coast and into the Severn? But it is more probable that the thorn was planted there by the priest of the nearby medieval chapel as an attraction to pilgrims and a distraction to his loneliness.

This building is now known as Chapel Cottages, and stands as a buttress of the sea wall where the land bends into the river, and where the main channel of the Severn curves towards the chapel. Navigational lights stand on the shore beside the building and they remind us that Thomas, Lord Berkeley, who founded the chapel in the fourteenth century, was a practical man. He gave 'competent lands' to maintain a priest to sing there, and under his heirs the house became a chantry until the Reformation. It stands exactly opposite the monastic chapel of Woolaston across the river. The chapel served the secular purpose of being a guide to shipping and a landmark to sailors.

One of its priests wrote this Latin phrase about the parish of Hill: 'Hieme mala, aestate molesta, nunquam bona'— evil in winter, grievous in summer, and never good. But the holy thorn is not the only flower to bloom here in midwinter, in January I have seen the grass of the sea wall studded with daisies, and have even put my foot on five of them, for there is a saying in parts of Gloucestershire that if you can put your foot over five daisies then spring is here. The gladdon, or stinking iris, grows in the hedges hereabouts, where on account of its brilliant orange berries it is sometimes gathered for Christmas decorations.

The chapel building has undergone many changes, but the four walls now standing, bleak and angular against the Severn, would appear to be those of the original house. After the Reformation the chapel became a farmhouse, and only comparatively recently was it converted into cottages. Mrs. Bennett of the 'Windbound' tells me that her mother remembered the time when the whole of the top floor was beautifully panelled in black oak, which was taken out along with the fine old oak staircase.

The gardens of Chapel Cottages are the only ones I have seen along the river where the plentiful seaweed is used as manure. Shepherdine, or Shipperdine as its inhabitants prefer to spell it, takes its name from the Danish ships which beached here in Anglo-Saxon days. These Vikings must have led a gipsy existence in the heart of Saxon England, protected by the Severn and its tides, and hedged in by the Forest of Horwood.

The New Inn, Sheperdine, better known to locals and intimates as the 'Windbound,' crouches under the sea wall well below the level of the highest tides, which lap only a few feet away from its walls. The house received its strange name the 'Windbound' from the bargees of the old coal barges, for this was one of the few inns on the river where there were stout iron mooring-posts inside the sea wall, to which the bargee could moor his barge while he drunk himself silly. These drinking bouts, when inns were open all day and half the night, often lasted for three or four days, and when the barge arrived late up-river the bargee made the excuse that he had been windbound.

The most fascinating visitor who has ever come to the 'Windbound' was in very truth windbound. He was a 'hawk penguin' who in spite of this strange name was one of our own native birds, either a guillemot or possibly a razor-bill. He was carried over the sea wall in a storm and was cherished for some days in a pen, where, unfamiliar with the ways of human kind, he was bold enough to bite the hand that fed him, but he died 'because we did not know the right food to give him.' He is more likely to have sickened through being deprived of his natural drink, which is salt-water, since these birds spend their lives on the open sea and only sojourn on land to breed.

In 1910 there was such a violent storm in the Severn that the tide came over the sea wall, pouring down the chimneys of the 'Windbound,' flooding the bar to a depth of four feet. Nominally this was a comparatively low tide, being a twenty-one-footer, but there were two days of unrelenting gale behind it. Only measurements can give any idea of the power of a wind behind the tide in the restricted area of the lower Severn; even above Sharpness a twenty-six-foot tide has reached the thirty-four-foot mark when the wind has been in the 'wrong quarter.' Not only was the 'Windbound' flooded, but the tide flowed two miles inland, floating wheelbarrows and timber away from their appointed places.

From Sheperdine the main stream of the river crosses its bed to the opposite shore, so that it flows two miles away from the sea wall and offers its fullest scope to the basket fisherman. Many years ago an attempt was made to introduce this type of fishing in the mouth of the Shannon, and Thomas Haines, a Severn water-bailiff, made models of kipes, butts, and foreweels for an exhibition in Ireland. The type of basket fishing on this side of the river as opposed to the putcher, or putt, across the water, presents a problem from the fisherman's point of view in the life-cycle of the salmon. The putcher being loosely woven catches nothing but salmon, or perhaps on rare occasions a good-sized sea fish. The foreweel on the end of the kipe catches everything that swims into it, so that at one time salmon pinks going down to the sea were caught in the foreweels as thick as whitebait. Bucketfuls of these tiny fish were taken from the baskets at the beginning of summer only to be thrown away, and every one of these fish, small as a minnow, was prevented from becoming a salmon, who in the course of nature would one day return to the river. An ingenious method of overcoming this destruction was devised by leaving the stopper at the end of the foreweel open for a fortnight in the month of May, when everything passed through the basket except the adult salmon, which lodged there.

Aust Cliff closes in on the broad expanse of Severn and, as it juts out towards the headland of Beachley, one knows that here is the natural end of the Severn long before reaching it. Oldbury Pill prevents one walking along the river bank and, as it is unbridged and at low tide deep mud, it compels one to visit the village of Oldbury. This stream, unlike most rivers which are blessed with ancient British names, was called the Rhine by our Saxon forbears, and while many a ditch in Somerset is called a reen, Oldbury still maintains the German .pronounciation. It has even survived two world wars, possibly because it is a dirty inconvenient stretch of water with nothing to commend it.

The chief glory of Oldbury-on-Severn is the Beauty of Worcester clematis, which flourishes abundantly on every cottage boasting a porch. He was a wise man who first introduced this commonest, loveliest, and most prolific of garden clematises to this village, for this plant alone makes a visit to Oldbury in late summer an unforgettable memory. Oldbury is one of several villages that cluster round the small town of Thornbury, which are linked together by an intricate maze of lanes. Along these lanes stands many a farmhouse glowing with hereditary prosperity and traditional pride, since for centuries the Thornbury villages have been renowned for their cider and their cheese. The strong apple-growing land that runs the length of Severn tide, now one side of the river now the other, in a narrow belt reappears again round Thornbury to produce a cider that is the natural complement to Double Gloucester cheese. Only English indifference to food, and to good cheese in particular, can explain the decline of Double Gloucester cheese on the English table; even in the county of its origin it is hard to come by. Double Gloucester is the king of English cheeses; akin to Cheddar, it excels that cheese in richness and in flavour as a vintage burgundy excels a cheap claret. In the days when Thornbury was remote even from Bristol, farmers were compelled to turn their milk into cheese or butter. Nowadays the milk is collected for them at the farmyard gate. But the tradition of good cheese-making still persists, and farmer and farmer's wife still win the appreciation of those, who like themselves, enjoy a good cheese. Double Gloucester is made between March and October and requires five days to make and eight weeks to mature. It is a round, flat cheese weighing thirty-three pounds. Single Gloucester undergoes a slightly different process; a lower degree of acidity is developed before vatting and the curd is not so firm and dry as that of its elder brother, and when made Single Gloucester weighs fourteen pounds.

One of my pleasantest memories of Thornbury is of attending a cider sale, held on the small lawn of an ivy-clad farmhouse. The garden was surrounded by apple trees in full bloom in promise of next autumn's cider press. You may have watched the work of an old master or a historic property sold under the hammer. The price soars in a matter of seconds; in a few minutes property, which has remained in the hands of a family for generations, is sold for a fortune. The auctioneer knows that there is so much money in the world, he is a shrewd judge of the length of his bidder's pockets, and he knows just about how far even a millionaire will go beyond £30,000.

But at a cider sale no man knows what he is buying until the cask has been broached and the sample tasted, and the entire afternoon between lunch and tea-time is spent in the disposal of a dozen or fifteen lots. The barrels are lined up on the lawn, there are three or four benches, a trestle-table, and a score of blue and puce china mugs. The auctioneer begins his flattering preamble about the cider and its maker, and while he talks his handy-man fills up the mugs with Lot 1. Mugs have been raised. 'What may I start at, gentlemen?' says the auctioneer, and diffidently suggests a price. A full half minute passes, every one drinks again, and a voice makes an opening bid forty per cent below that suggested by the auctioneer. The buyers are cider merchants and publicans, who will retail the casks in pints and quarts. They sip again and with each sip the price advances until it passes the auctioneer's mark. The auctioneer smiles and looks around for another smiling face, who relishes the drink in his mug above the rest of the company. He finds it in old gaffer Tom, who has put away more cider in his time than any one else present. He will open his mouth many times during the afternoon, but not to bid. He is still a fine figure of a man and now, nearly eighty years of age, he is a retired farm labourer, living with a widowed daughter on the old age pension. The cider sale for him is a golden afternoon's escape from the boredom of inactive old age.

The lot is sold and from time to time nuggets of Double Gloucester cheese are handed round to clean the palate. Old Thomas has a bold defiant face whose origins have not budged from the Thornbury district for many centuries. As you face him across the lawn, you wonder if that look came from a Saxon invader, or from an ancient Briton, who made a last stand on Severnside to survive, hid in some thicket, and hand on that look to old Tom. It is a cast of countenance one often sees upon old faces round Thornbury and nowhere else. Old Tom knows that he has not the wherewithal to bid for any of the lots, but he knows, too, that he has as much right to sample them as the next man. He has made cider, he has planted some of the trees that have helped to fill these casks, and certainly no one resents his presence. He is not alone for next him sits another veteran, who seems quite inconspicuous, for beside old Tom he is a timid drinker. He is a trifle deaf, and into his ear Tom confides his opinion of the varying merits of the ciders as they pass. In this Tom observes a strict mode of decorum, for he never comments on any cider while it remains under the auctioneer's hammer.

Cask after cask is sold and the sale winds up with one smaller than the rest, holding cider as rare as any to be tasted on Severnside. It is a blend of Foxwhelp or Kingston Black with another choice cider apple, and half a mug of it on top of two hours' steady drinking makes you feel that you have been quaffing nectar all the afternoon. It fetches a magnificent price and with it the sale ends.

'Best be getting along home,' says Tom to his companion, and reflects that, being the best part of a gallon of cider to the good, he can dispense for once with the humdrum ritual of drinking tea.

The town of Thornbury has a church with a beautiful Perpendicular tower and a castle, still in habitation, where Henry VIII and Anne Boleyn spent ten days of their honeymoon, having been compelled to stay here longer than they had intended, owing to an outbreak of plague in Bristol.

Thornbury lies a good way from the river, for not only were two thousand acres of Thornbury at one time rated for the repair of the sea wall, but a much greater area was liable to floods, which left stagnant water in the marshes. The Thornbury marshes were so unhealthy in the eighteenth century, that Samuel Rudder wrote of them: 'If any go from the hill country to reside there, such persons are usually attacked with a violent ague on their first settling, which emaciates them, and proves fatal in a little time.' Country people wore charms against the ague. Stukeley, the father of British archaeology, mentions in his *Itineraria Curiosa* the skull of a certain Roman lady named Julia Casta, which was kept in a summer-house in Cirencester. All the teeth of the skull had been stolen as amulets against ague. Who Julia Casta was we shall never know. In the Roman world she was very much of a provincial, but no doubt shone as a great lady in Roman-British society.

The ague of the Thornbury marshes retarded the development of this district throughout the centuries, and possibly the most amazing event that has happened here was the landing of the great whale, which occurred round about 1880, when Thornbury folk flocked down to watch Leviathan docked in Littleton Pill and dragged ashore by traction engines. My father, as a small boy, was amongst them, and when I was a small boy I never tired of asking him to tell me about the great whale of Thornbury. To me it was the more glorious for having really happened. This monster was no Jubertas, but a whale such as Captain Ahab might have chased half way across an ocean. There are few people around here to-day who remember seeing this whale, but old George of Framilode, who has seen everything worth seeing on Severn tide, saw him alive 'thrashing with his tail' above English Stones.

Before improved drainage robbed the Thornbury marshes of their indigenous character, they were the haunt of the herbalist and vegetable gatherer. The asparagus grew wild here, flourishing beside brackish water, and in spring country folk cut and gathered the buds which they sold in Bristol. Purslane, too, was gathered for the table, while the old women of Olveston lined their pockets by selling vervain, or *herba sacra*, a plant which had a great reputation for the cure of scrofula. In those days this disease was still known as the king's evil, since its cure was supposed to be effected by the royal touch. Kings and queens seem to have shown little aversion for touching the scrofulous cheeks of their subjects, and no doubt Charles I flattered himself into believing that this was an outward and visible sign of the 'divine right of kings.' Queen Anne touched the scrofulous cheeks of Samuel Johnson, when that great man was a child. Vervain was much in demand when the practice of the royal touch disappeared with the more aloof manners of the House of Hanover.

The great cliffs of Aust with those of Beachley across the

* F

river are composed of Rhaetic deposits, and are the tomb of extinct creatures who aimlessly roamed primitive seas, for here have been unearthed the remains of the icthyosaurus and plesiosaurus and the shark Hybodus. A more picturesque and recent loss to the fauna of Aust is the swallow-tail butterfly. The draining of the marshes deprived the caterpillar of this magnificent insect of much of its natural food. It was seen here in the middle of the last century, when the zeal of the butterfly hunter brought about its irrevocable extinction.

At Aust, though this is a point on which minor historians quibble, St. Augustine met the Welsh bishops. Aust and not Down Ampney is certainly the more probable venue of the ecclesiastics, for Aust is a landmark, and by crossing the waters of the Severn to meet the Roman missionary the Welsh clergy were performing a symbolic act of homage to Augustine. One may picture these Welshmen as they crossed the river, eager, after their long isolation in the faith, and excited at meeting an envoy from the capital of Christianity, while Augustine, for all his saintliness, was also a man and was probably a little piqued to find that Britain was not wholly pagan and that the seed, which is the word of God, had already fallen on stony places among the Welsh mountains and taken root there. The hospitable, friendly Welshmen were no doubt a little chilled by the austere, aloof, and slightly suspicious priest from Rome. Augustine quickly discovered that the Welsh church observed the great feasts of the church on days which were not identical with those in the Roman calendar. The Welsh bishops to their eternal credit were not overawed and were loud in their insistence on following the dates which had been handed down to them from their fathers. Angry, obstinate, disappointed men recrossed the Severn. Welsh nonconformity had begun while England was being baptized, and Augustine rode away from Aust bitterly preferring the unconverted heathen to the heretics from Wales.

XV. THE FOREST SHORE

A little way above Beachley the Severn is two miles wide, yet the Beachley peninsula, shaped by the main streams of Severn and Wye, sprawls like the claw of a lobster to within a mile of Aust Cliff. This arm of land is one of the three contributory causes to the Severn Bore, since high tides and the gently shelving river bed would not be sufficient to create the Bore without this natural breakwater, stemming a tide on flood and checking its natural resilient backwash to the sea.

The Severn between Sharpness and Beachley is a tidal lake ten miles long with an enormous capacity for holding the exceptional tides, which are forced into it through a relatively narrow passage. A mile from Beachley Point the isthmus of the peninsula is so narrow that a man might stand in the centre of it and throw a stone into either the Severn or the Wye. This is a fascinating spot on the shape of Britain, for the two rivers rise within a mile of each other on Plynlimon, yet from the hour they have ceased to tumble down the mount of their origin their characters are wholly different. But here, invaded by the sea, they share something in common as they flow between banks of muddy ooze and seaweed that festoons the rocks.

The two rivers are united in the anonymous oblivion of the sea at St. Twrog's chapel beyond Beachley Point, where from the river cliff an outcrop of seaweed-covered rock descends to rise in a miniature St. Michael's Mount, some two hundred yards from land. It is something of a penance to make the pilgrimage to St. Twrog's over thick seaweed, slippery rocks, and patches of mud. It is not to be recommended to the elderly archaeologist, or to those who are ignorant or nervous of the tides. The rock is crowned by the ruins of the chapel of which only two walls, four and five yards long, stand ten feet high at right angles to one another. The longer wall holds the doorway of the chapel, which gapes like an eye grown vacant with age at sky and sea. The effect is somewhat marred by the navigational light which towers inside and above the ruin, but this the beholder can hardly resent when he considers that the chapel in ancient days served as a light and beacon to mariners. As you approach the chapel up cascades of wet seaweed you wonder how the building can stand above the high-tide mark, yet around the ruin, in defiance of the sea, the ground is green with grass, thrift, the sea-aster, wild garlic, and other valiant weeds and flowers. Simeon Stylites on his pillar was hardly more isolated from his fellow men than the anchorite who ministered in this ancient chapel. If nothing but seaweed grew upon the rock the contrast would not be so great, but you look from the tiny patch of impoverished vegetation at your feet to the fertile abundance of field and forest, to the pasture, to the golden cornlands and the mighty oaks of Dean, and the grass at your feet is but a withered bloom, stolen from a garden. There is, however, a lonely gaiety about this rock, and its ancient sanctity has a mysticism all its own, which takes possession of the solitary visitor. You may stand here and behold the sea and sky, and a distant and more intimate prospect of earth at her fairest, and comprehend something of the imagery of the Bible. Here man lived and prayed, asking little or nothing of his fellow men, and nature fed him. If he was too un-practical to fish for himself, there was often a salmon or a sea fish stranded on the rocks or in the pools at low tide, and there were plenty of eels. There was always the tide to ease the monotony of time; the water would rise to within a few inches of the threshold of the chapel and would ebb leaving several acres of rock, seaweed, and a little sandy beach where the anchorite might wander to look for what God had brought him in the shape of a stranded or pool-imprisoned fish.

Almost nothing is known of the history of the chapel and the scanty remains of its architecture defy classification. On the ordnance survey map the chapel is called St. Twrog's, but according to Sir Robert Atkyns, the earliest historian of Gloucestershire, the chapel was dedicated to St. Tecla, who,

A NEAT JOB IN BASKET WORK: BUTTS ON THE BERKELEY SHORE

he tells us, was martyred in the year 47 and was the first Christian martyr of her sex. The further extremity of St. Twrog's, or St. Tecla's, is at low tide the true confluence of the Severn and the Wye, and is the end of the Severn as a river. This patch of water, where the rivers commingle with the sea, is known as the Treacle.

Beachley was once part of Tidenham, whose boundaries extended for fifteen miles, twelve of which were moated by the Severn and Wye. Fishing in Tidenham is nothing like so extensive as it was a thousand years ago. According to Domesday Book, the abbey of Bath, who owned the manor, held eleven fisheries, in addition to a further forty-two worked by villeins. Catches were brought across the dangerous estuary of the Severn on the ebb tide and up the Bristol Avon on the flood tide, probably by coracle, and cargoes included herrings and porpoise for the monks of Bath.

The majority of these fisheries were in the Wye, on which there is still some stopping-boat fishing, but there is only one basket fishery on Tidenham's ancient Severn boundary at the end of Sedbury Cliffs. Near here grows a patch of that beautiful and unusual plant the sea-pea. The main stream of Severn flows under Sedbury Cliffs, through a channel known by the descriptive and uninviting name of Slime Road. The cliffs are steep, red, and sunless and their feet are strewn with vast flat slabs of stone. Here and there one finds the imprint of an ammonite and in contrast the spoor of the otter, fresh in the mud of the receding tide.

Sedbury Cliffs are for the geologist and the musician, for this melancholy place has a music all its own. There is an orchestration of wind and tide, and from the dry cliffs at intervals comes the sound of running water, it is last year's red beech leaves cascading to the foot of the cliff. Sea birds seldom add their voices to this inanimate music, and the only bird that I have met here was a solitary twite, who twittered continuously as he danced ahead of me, flying from rock to rock for half a mile, never allowing me to draw level or pass him.

The red cliffs of the Severn, so old that the age of their rocks can be measured in hundreds of millions of years, guide the course of the tidal stream to the sea. The Mythe and Wainload, Garden Cliff and Hock Cliff, have mapped the river, forcing it to writhe in its bed into those serpentines, which in the course of time have become so entrancing to the eye. Yet only at Aust and Sedbury do these great cliffs stand in opposition to one another, a gateway to stream and tide. They give an intimacy to the river, despite the Severn's intercourse with the sea, and without Aust and Sedbury, of little interest in themselves, the tide-way would be deprived of much of its individuality.

Tide and stream are powerless against these cliffs and the other cliffs of Severn, but elsewhere within these ancient confines the tide and stream gamble with the land upon their shore. To the north of Sedbury the land has been increasing for centuries, most noticeably within the last three hundred years, but in the last few years the tide has shown an inclination to return and reclaim what it has leased to the land.

Lydney church is far from the river, but a large ship was launched from the piece of ground adjoining the church-yard, known as the Turret, probably in Tudor times. Two ships of Cromwell's navy were launched in Lydney Pill; built of forest oak and iron, the first of these, the *Forester*, was of three hundred and six tons with twenty-two guns. The *Princess*, the successor to this ship in the stocks, was a larger vessel with more than double the complement of men and armament.

With oak and iron at hand Lydney might have become a naval dockyard, but seven years later with the Restoration Daniel Furser, the master shipwright, wrote to Samuel Pepys at the Admiralty that 'Lydney is not so fit a place now for building a ship as formerly, on account of the growing of the sands, not known in man's memory before.' He suggested the now deserted Cone Pill, a few miles below the town, as a better shipyard and it was here that he built and launched the *St. David*, a frigate of six hundred and thirty-eight tons. But Lydney has never recovered from 'the growing of the sands.'

The forest stone with which Lydney is built is hard, drab, and sunless. It has robbed the architect of any latent inspiration and taken the heart out of the builder. Lydney has none of the atmosphere of a country town, for her agricultural environment could only give lustre to a small village. Lydney was once on Severn's bank, hemmed in by the forest, whose stream, the Cannop, extended into a winding pill. Lydney Pill, like Bullo, provided an easy and natural exit for the products of the forest, and before the railways were built there were few coalfields in Britain that possessed greater facilities for export than the Forest of Dean. Lydney Pill, having outlived its usefulness as a shipyard, was promoted to the dignity of a harbour. Its entrance to the Severn was sealed by lock gates and the meandering pill transformed into a long, narrow dock. As late as 1890 the harbour was thronged with small craft with as many as three hundred vessels in the dock, and fifteen to a score of them would leave on every tide. They were mostly sailing vessels and all carried coal to the little ports on the coasts of Somerset and north Devon. Those were leisurely days when a bargemaster often had to wait his turn for a month or even six weeks for his cargo. The railway, preferring its own methods of transport and proud of the new bridge it had built across the Severn, slowly strangled the life of the little port. To-day there are not above half a dozen barges in the harbour, with the result that freshwater fish, among them carp, have found a happy haven there. Their only enemies, apart from local rod-and-line fishermen, are the otters, who encouraged by good living have brought up families in an orchard wilderness close to the station.

Lydney, despite its appearance, is a proud place and is immensely proud of the pier. A stranger, if he did not utterly ignore it, might affront Lydney by calling it by some other name, for this snub-nosed piece of solid masonry does not jut further than a few paces into the river, and its butt end serves as a wall for the harbour lock. The main channel of the Severn flows against the opposite shore, and the little port has only a distant view of the shipping that passes to Sharpness. In early spring the pier is thronged with elverers, since the harbour's mouth is Lydney's only chance of catching an elver, and is the elvers' first port of call inside the Severn. After their long swim across the Atlantic, the elvers, instinctively thirsting for fresh water, and finding the lower Severn still too salty, crowd to the pier head of Lydney harbour. Elvering here has none of the grace and finish of elvering as seen on the Gloucester and Tewkesbury reaches of the river. The tide is too boisterous here for a net of cheese muslin, instead the elvers are caught with a meat-sieve, borrowed for the day, and woe betide the husband or son who comes home without either meat-sieve or elvers.

A long spinney fringes Huntsman's Cliff above Lydney harbour. The shore under here is of red stone, grey mud, and an occasional fleck of green lias. Indeed one might almost imagine that the Roman found the idea for his mosaics on the Severn floor. A weir of putcheons splays out from the shore under Cliff Farm, while the fisherman's hut hangs like a nest among the bushes of the cliff, where a rough but carefully built stairway, known as Jacob's Ladder, links it with the wood above and the river below. The hut, which is no bigger than a small living-room, has a chimney that seems to belong as much to the cliff as it does to the building. There is an air of healthy shabbiness about the place that comes not of neglect but of hard work. It is the perfect hide-out for a pirate or a prophet, for it has never known the desolating thoroughness of woman's toil, and one would as soon expect to see a line of washing hanging there as from the battlements of Berkeley Castle. The empty wicker putcheons, stacked against its outside wall, give to the hut a clean, wholesome atmosphere and an air of magic and mystery. But the wood has another magic all its own when April declares that every other tree in it is the wild cherry. This tree is common enough in the forest, but in no part of Dean does it grow so

plentifully as here, upon what was once its natural boundary.
Indeed, were the spinney to be thinned of its oak and thorn
it would become an orchard of wild cherry-trees and make a
natural paradise of the top of Jacob's Ladder.

Jacob's Ladder fishery is owned by the Biddles, who live
at Cliff Farm close to the top of the ladder, and when the
cherry is in blossom you may see father and son weaving their
salmon putts on the turf overlooking the cliff, just outside
their barton gate. The Biddles are farmer-fishermen and,
with all the spring-tide labour on the farm, they find time to
weave enough putts to fill their weir. They are probably
the champion putt-makers on the Severn, for in addition to
the essential routine on the farm they are able to weave as
many as twenty-five putts in a day; and as their weir holds
three hundred putts, half of which have to be replenished each
season, they are able to furnish their weir by a week's work.

This weir is about the smallest on the river, but is possibly
the best situated, for it stands in a 'gutter' draining out of
Wellhouse Bay, the finest salmon pool in the Severn. A
tremendous current of water passes through this weir and as
many as twenty-five fish have been taken here in one day.
There is an especially strong flow of water for the first half
hour of the ebb of the tide, it is known as Tate's Gush and
brings the greatest number of fish to the putts, and more fish
are taken at the week-ends while there is no fishing in Wellhouse Bay.

Hugh Biddle, while he was weaving a putt, told me that the
right to a basket fishery dated from the reign of King John,
when it was enacted that wherever a basket fishery was in
operation in the year of Magna Charta it might persist in
perpetuity.

The Severn is continually adding and subtracting land to
and from the New Grounds below Lydney harbour, causing
elation or vexation to those who farm them. Since Daniel
Furser wrote to Pepys about the 'growing of the sands' in
front of Lydney, the Severn has added about a mile of now
fertile pasture to the foreshore. About ten years ago the river,

as though regretting her gift of land, set about reclaiming it by outflanking the old sea wall and necessitating the building of a new one. But still the loss continues, and the spring tides of April 1944 were specially destructive, when the river advanced at high water to Lydney station and an acre of ground was carried away in a week. The task of erosion is an easy one. The land seems firm enough, there are eight feet of deep rich soil, but below it lies a bed of river sand, which the river undermines and washes away, leaving the soil to crumble like cake. It is a tragedy to watch the disappearance of so much fine grass, for the turf here is as fine as any to be seen on the lawns of Oxford's colleges. Indeed, the absence of wild flowers detracts from the interest of a solitary walk. The only colouring to this turf is the wings of dead birds, mallard, teal, curlew, and magpie, washed up by the tide. But this fine turf before long gives place to mud and ooze upon which the grass makes a tentative foothold. Here the ground lies two feet below the level of the rest of the land, for this is new ground in process of being built up from the soil eroded a mile or so up-river. Each high tide leaves a thin alluvial layer of mud. The growth of such land from the farmer's point of view is something in the nature of a life insurance policy which he may never live to enjoy, since it takes thirty years for these new grounds to mature to valuable pasture. During their growth cows wander out upon them to crop the thin grass, but winter tides effectively kill what grass there is and nature has to begin over again in the spring. You may wander over these level, muddy grounds to find yourself in a maze when a pill with its primeval mud-banks bars your progress. Then taking another direction the walker finds himself on the bank of another pill, lost to the eye on the level ground until he is on top of it. In exasperation you may have to walk a mile to cover a few yards. Under such conditions, when you find the pill narrowing, you are tempted to make a leap, but the take-off is slippery and the landing even more treacherous. The water in the bottom of the pill may only be six inches deep and a foot wide, but the gully is a formidable one. Once a missed foothold caused me a six-foot fall; the ground on landing could not have been softer or muddier. I got up without a bruise, plastered from head to foot.

How much the land has increased round Aylburton Warth may be seen in the buried run of a putcheon weir, the tops of whose firmly planted stakes are still showing above the grass. It is a sad sight, for in these days it does not take much to break the heart of a salmon fisherman who fishes with putts, and a calamity of this kind may spell the end of a dynasty of fishermen.

One may regain the river bank at Plitsterwine close to Guscar Rocks, which have prevented any landward growth into the river. These rocks at low tide are an archipelago of seaweed-covered islands, and it is here that the Bore is popularly, but erroneously, supposed to begin. It would be hard to give any landmark as the beginning of the Bore. It rises almost imperceptibly between here and Sedbury, and because it is never more than a two-foot wave is accounted no marvel so near to the open sea.

Guscar is locally known as the Grange Rocks from the nearby Grange of Woolaston. The rocks cover several acres and carry a heavy crop of seaweed, which in thriftier times was gathered as manure. Indeed, so much seaweed should encourage someone to grow hops in Woolaston.

One of the great tragedies of the river occurred off these rocks in the last century, when a Norwegian four-masted windjammer entered the river too early on the tide and was overwhelmed. The captain's wife and small son were drowned and are buried in Woolaston churchyard. John Biddle, of Plitsterwine Farm, sheltered the captain and his crew, and received the bodies of his dead. The Norwegians remained with him for a fortnight. What greater tragedy could overtake a man in the fullness of life than for him to lose his wife, his son, and his ship through his own ignorance or error of judgment, and after it to live for a fortnight amid the mild surroundings of Plitsterwine, within sight of the treacherous river?

But something remained to that Norwegian captain, for when he took his leave of John Biddle he gave the farmer the one possession of value remaining to him, his gold watch-chain. I never met John Biddle, though he lived to be over eighty, but somehow I like him for receiving such a gift from a man who had lost so much. A lesser man would have refused the gift, and the Norwegian captain would have gone away poor indeed, knowing that he was pitied. This chain is now a treasured heirloom of the Biddles, and a woman and her son, who lie among the Woolaston dead, are not forgotten.

Inshore from Guscar the land has altered little with the centuries as may be seen from the great oaks—giants who have outlived this corner of the forest that begat them. In their solitude they are as fine as any oaks in England. The mistletoe here and for the next two miles grows in great profusion and abundance, not as an orchard parasite, but on the hawthorn. There is a common belief, which receives the support of reference books, that the mistletoe grows on the oak. If it grows naturally on the oak it would do so here, where there are oaks a-plenty, but it clings to the hawthorn, some- times transforming it to an evergreen tree in winter. I have peered through scores of oaks in the bareness of December between here and Sedbury without finding a mistletoe upon them, though thorn-trees on either side were festooned with the golden bough. The fruit-eating birds propagate the mistletoe, when they wipe the gummy seeds from their beaks upon the branches of trees, and once it has taken hold the mistletoe will live until the tree dies. Perhaps the hands of a Druid were needed to graft the mistletoe upon the oak.

The high embankment of the railway line, which serves as a sea wall against the highest tides, hides Woolaston Grange from the river. The Grange belonged to Tintern Abbey and is now consequently free of tithes. It is a gaunt farmhouse contrasting oddly with its farm buildings, for one of the barns is the old monastic chapel. The Grange was one of those dependencies of great abbeys where hard work, rather than

TIDE RUNNING THROUGH PUTCHEON WEIR AT JACOB'S LADDER

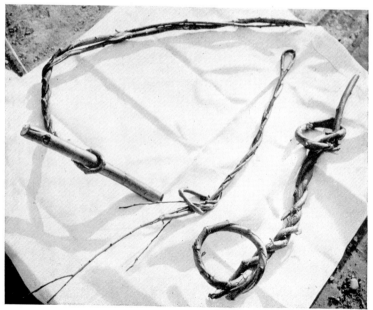

Photo: P. C. Palmer

Left: ROD AND PIN. *Right:* APSES

intensive prayer, was the order of the day. The abbot looked
to a full granary and plenty of fresh fish in Lent and on fast
days. The abbots of Tintern made a practice of employing
a daring rapscallion or two from among the forest men to act
as poachers of the king's deer on their behalf. Many a stag
must have come down here to soil himself in the mud of
Severn, and the wise poacher preferred to kill his animal as
near to the Grange as possible.

There is a low, red cliff below the Grange, the reddest on
Severn shore, for it is as bright as any mellow brick wall that
shelters a manor garden, and is an impressive sight when
reflected in the water at high tide. At any time of the year
the cliff is the most vivid patch of colour in the landscape,
and glows with exotic warmth on the dullest day in winter,
so that whenever I have passed here I have turned round
several times to admire this cliff from afar.

Beyond the cliff is Horsepill Putcheons and when the putts
are out of season they may be seen stacked round the black
hut of the fisherman, which they transform into the fantastic
likeness of a medieval castle made of wicker. This is a small
one-man fishery holding four hundred putts, which involves
an outlay of over £100 for a season of four months. A putt
is only allowed by licence to remain in the water from 15th
April to 15th August. Thus with two tides in the twenty-four
hours each putt has a chance at very long odds of catching a
fish two hundred and forty-four times in a season. A putt
will last for two years, and half the putts are renewed each
year. This is a great expense for the independent fisherman,
who on this weir pays £40 in rent, £11 in poor rate, and
£16, or £4 a hundred, in tax on his putts. Two hundred
putts at ten putts a day represents three weeks of hard work.
Nor is the putt made for nothing, for though the basket is
woven of hazel and willow, and looks slender enough, it uses
3s. worth of material and costs at least 1s. worth of labour
to produce. With almost another 1s. in tax, exclusive of rent
and rates, 5s. must be spent on a basket, which may catch
nothing in a whole season.

Below Horsepills, hidden by the railway line, stands the Broadstone, which with another similar stone high up on the hill is the solitary monument of prehistoric Britain in this part of the country. It is a flat, upright monolith, standing eight feet high, heavily lichened. Time has robbed this stone of its significance and also of its setting, for the railway line separates it from the Severn. But it still stands to show that the Severn hereabouts has not shifted her bed much in the past three thousand years, for to-day it is not more than two hundred yards from the river.

It is the oldest monument on Severn tide and may have witnessed the tragedy of Sabrina, daughter of Locrine, who, pursued by 'her enragèd stepdame Guendolen,' drowned herself in the river to which she bequeathed her name. The stone was obviously erected in the river's honour and may at one time have been associated with the cult of the Severn river god, Nodens. The temple of Nodens is marked 'outpost' on the ordnance survey, and stands above Aylburton, between the village and Lydney.

On my way to the temple a sparrow-hawk hovered in the windless sky. He engrossed my attention and that of a man working in a field, and created by his presence a link between us. The unseen prey outmanœuvred the bird. There is no gesture of frustration among birds equal to that of a hawk as he swerves from the hover into the exasperation of flight.

'Missed him,' said the man, and we smiled as we might have done at a cricket match. I told him that I was on my way to the hill of Nodens. He pointed out the way to me and then stood still as a countryman will when he is about to tell you something of importance.

'The river once came to the foot of that hill, for my father dug pure Severn sand at the foot of the slope, just below the temple.'

Geologists and archaeologists may state their opinions in a less straightforward manner, while those who take the gently sloping path from the main road to the foot of the hill may shake their heads. But they must remember that once the main stream of the river, controlled by current and tide, turned away from the creek, the ground on which they tread was filled with the erosions of two steep and considerable slopes. The falling of the leaf every autumn through many generations of trees, the thunderstorms, the floods that have swelled the forest brooks to overflowing, and the frosts and thaws of a millennium and a half, have done their work over a wider span that that allowed to the restricted vision of man.

The ravine forks immediately below the temple, whose walls still stand three feet above ground and are built of forest stone well cemented together. As recently as the eighteenth century these walls were eight feet high, and it is surprising that this temple should have been denuded in so romantic a setting in an age when the gentry were wasting their money in ornamenting their estates with pseudo-classical temples and grottoes, for this ruin stands in Lydney Park. The situation of the temple is as charming as any in England, standing on the edge of a grassy plateau with a deep ravine on either hand, whose slopes are covered in well-matured timber. These trees are part of the native woodland of the Forest of Dean, garlanded with great bunches of mistletoe. Indeed the only alien among them is the Spanish chestnut, brought here by the Romans along with the fallow deer which still graze around the temple. The view from the temple is filled with the broad river lands and beyond the equally broad river, for both the Severn and the intervening ground are two miles wide. To-day the flood head of the Bore runs up along the Berkeley sea wall four miles away from here and is almost imperceptible at Lydney harbour. When we consider the changes that the Severn can bring about in a lifetime and then attempt to speculate on this work during fifty generations, during which time it was unconfined by any sea wall, we may then imagine the tide gushing into the creek at the foot of the hill of Nodens, filling the hearts of those who beheld it with wonder and religious ecstacy.

The temple of Nodens is the most intimate relic in the whole of Roman Britain. Nodens is more than a name and his solitary shrine is more than an ordinary ruin. The ground-plan is rectangular and covers an area thirty yards by twenty-four yards, and is unique for its period in having six side chapels. The building dates from the fourth century A.D. when much care was lavished upon it. The floor of the temple is now covered with turf, which hides and protects its tessellated pavements. Scores of these pavements have been discovered in Gloucestershire, mostly in Cirencester and on the Cotswolds. They are mosaics built of small cubes of coloured local stone, whose reds and greens were mined in the river bed and cliffs of the Severn.

The Romans were not an artistic people. The culture of ancient Greece was only theirs by assimilation, and the ancestors of the Italian Renaissance were that fascinating race of image-makers the primitive Etruscans. The patterns on Roman pavements are ingenious things, but they are as formal and precise as their language and grammar. They usually depict themes of classical mythology and, when unearthed, are only to be preserved with great trouble and expense, since skilled Italian labour is required to reset them. We may regret, however, that the pavements of the god Nodens are hidden from view, for he is represented on the floor of his temple surrounded by salmon and sea serpents, or more probably conger eels, a fish greatly esteemed by the Romans. He is also shown rising from his river wearing a crown. He is in a chariot drawn by four horses and is accompanied by Tritons bearing coracle paddles. In his person the god Nodens resembles Neptune, except that, unlike the sea god, he has no beard.

The worship of the god Nodens probably did not extend beyond Severn tide and the hills of Dean and Monmouth. He was a local and tribal god and the initials D.M. (Deus Maximus) indicate that here he was all-important as the greatest god of the Silures. Some racial strain of this great tribe of ancient Britons still persists after two thousand years in the dilutions of our island history. They were forest folk and the forest preserved them from Roman colonization and the pacification, which left the Briton to the east of the Severn an easy prey to the Saxon invader. They were protected by Severn tide and their dense woodlands offered no open battle-ground to Saxon arms. They were spared the annihilation of the battle of Dyrham. The Saxons were cattle men preferring the open grasslands. The Silurian was a hunter, a fisherman, and a skilled iron miner. He hunted the boar and the red deer, and his skill as a hunting man made him a dangerous and unpredictable foe. The Saxon failed to absorb or liquidate him and when Danish Canute came to the throne he gave the forest a charter written in Danish in the year 1018, upholding the Verderer's Court which has persisted until to-day.

The Norman Conquest, which revolutionized rural England, left the forest comparatively unmolested, since it offered the Conqueror one of his favourite hunting grounds, and as it was a royal forest the inhabitants of Dean were spared much of the degradation of petty feudalism. They saw a succession of English kings in their more pleasant moods, followed by the pageantry of their retinues, as they chased the wild red deer through the forest oaks.

A Plantagenet king, it is uncertain whether it was Edward I or Edward III, took forest miners with him on his Scottish wars. They were the first sappers in the British Army, and proved so useful in undermining the walls of Berwick-upon-Tweed that their services were rewarded by the privilege of Free Miners. A man born in the hundred of St. Briavels, who works for a year and a day in a mine, may register as a Free Miner and is still allowed to stake a claim in the forest to mine on his own account.

The bare outline of the forest's history is endorsed by the old proverb: 'Happy the eye 'twixt Severn and Wye.' Here you will still meet the lineal descendant of the ancient Briton; he is neither English nor Welsh, but as British as his ancestors who worshipped Nodens.

The Bore was a manifestation of the divinity of the river god, and his priests, once they had learnt to foretell the time of the arrival of the sacred wave, gained the confidence of simple men. The name of Nodens has been preserved in three inscriptions, which show that the river god held great power over men's minds as a god of health and healing. We have a fascinating glimpse into the somewhat familiar and materialistic relationship that existed between the god and one of his votaries in the following inscription:

DEVO NODENTI SILULANUS ANILUM PERDEDIT DEMEDIAM
PARTEM DONAVIT NODENTI INTER QUIBUS NOMEN SENICIANI
NULLIS PETMITTAS SANITATEM DONEC PERFERAT USQUE
TEMPLUM NODENTIS.

These words were scratched on metal, Latin being the only literate language of the age: 'To the god Nodens Silulanus has lost a ring and dedicated half (the value of the ring) to Nodens. Among those called Senicianus permit no health until he bring it to the temple of Nodens.'

Words which have the terseness of a notice in the window of a country police-station. Silulanus is a very human personality as he curses his enemy and bargains with his god. He never recovered his ring, which strangely enough was found at Silchester in the year 1785. We hear no more of Nodens. He was the god of good luck and as such he probably persisted in the folklore of the forest, and long after the Latin tongue was forgotten his name was still remembered, until the river slowly wandered away from his shrine among the woods.

INDEX

INDEX

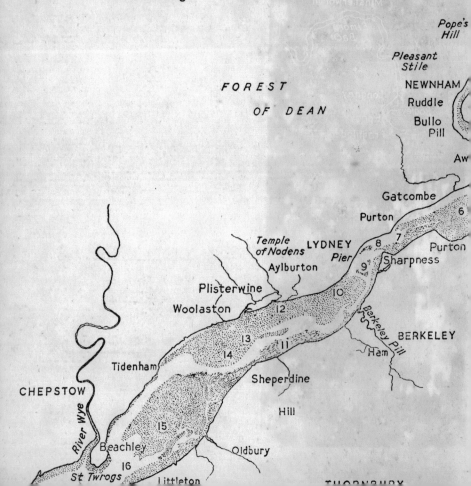

1 Longney Sand
2 Unla Water
3 Pimlico Sand
4 Garden Cliff
5 The Noose
6 Frampton Sand
7 Severn Bridge
8 Wellhouse Bay
9 The Prinn
10 Saniger Sand
11 Hills Flats
12 Lydney Sand
13 Guscar Rocks
14 Sheperdine Sands
15 Oldbury Sands
16 Aust Passage

FOREST

OF DEAN

Pope's
Hill

Pleasant
Stile

NEWNHAM
Ruddle

Bullo
Pill

Aw

Gatcombe

Purton

Temple
of Nodens   LYDNEY
Aylburton   Pier

8   7

9

Purton

Sharpness

Plisterwine

Woolaston

12

10

Berkeley Pill

BERKELEY

13

11

Ham

14

Tidenham

Sheperdine

CHEPSTOW

Hill

15

River Wye

Beachley

16

Oldbury

St Twrogs   Littleton

THORNBURY